OCCASIONAL
P A P E R

Heads We Win

The Cognitive Side of Counterinsurgency (COIN)

David C. Gompert

Prepared for the Office of the Secretary of Defense

Approved for public release; distribution unlimited

 NATIONAL DEFENSE RESEARCH INSTITUTE

The research described in this report was prepared for the Office of the Secretary of Defense (OSD). The research was conducted in the RAND National Defense Research Institute, a federally funded research and development center sponsored by the OSD, the Joint Staff, the Unified Combatant Commands, the Department of the Navy, the Marine Corps, the defense agencies, and the defense Intelligence Community under Contract W74V8H-06-C-0002.

Library of Congress Cataloging-in-Publication Data

Gompert, David C.
    Heads we win : the cognitive side of counterinsurgency (COIN) / David C. Gompert.
        p. cm.
    Includes bibliographical references.
    ISBN 978-0-8330-4021-3 (pbk. : alk. paper)
    1. Counterinsurgency—Psychological aspects. 2. Jihad. 3. Terrorism—Prevention. 4. United States—Military policy—21st century. I. Title. II. Title: Cognitive side of counterinsurgency.

U241.G65 2006
355.02'18—dc22

2007003864

The RAND Corporation is a nonprofit research organization providing objective analysis and effective solutions that address the challenges facing the public and private sectors around the world. RAND's publications do not necessarily reflect the opinions of its research clients and sponsors.

RAND® is a registered trademark.

Published 2007 by the RAND Corporation
1776 Main Street, P.O. Box 2138, Santa Monica, CA 90407-2138
1200 South Hayes Street, Arlington, VA 22202-5050
4570 Fifth Avenue, Suite 600, Pittsburgh, PA 15213-2665
RAND URL: http://www.rand.org/
To order RAND documents or to obtain additional information, contact
Distribution Services: Telephone: (310) 451-7002;
Fax: (310) 451-6915; Email: order@rand.org

Preface

This paper is one of the first outputs of the RAND Corporation's research project for the U.S. Department of Defense on how to improve U.S. counterinsurgency (COIN) capabilities. It should be of interest to the U.S. government and other countries and organizations now rethinking COIN strategies and retooling COIN capabilities in view of developments since September 11, 2001, as well as to scholars trying to understand continuity and change in this field.

The larger RAND project of which this is a part will yield a stream of interim products during its course. It will culminate in a final report that draws on that stream of work. Thus, this particular report can and should be read both as an output, in and of itself, and as a piece of a larger picture of COIN that is taking shape.

The topic, cognitive capabilities for COIN, is one that has not been analyzed heavily. Indeed, a reason for this paper is that the topic has not received enough attention, given the emphasis on technology, territorial control, and organization that characterizes U.S. COIN strategy and analysis. Thus, the author's purposes are to fuel debate and stimulate more research on an important yet neglected aspect of COIN.

This analysis was sponsored by the Combating Terrorism Technology Task Force of the U.S. Department of Defense and conducted within the International Security and Defense Policy Center of the RAND National Defense Research Institute, a federally funded research and development center sponsored by the Office of the Secretary of Defense, the Joint Staff, the Unified Combatant Commands, the Department of the Navy, the Marine Corps, the defense agencies, and the defense Intelligence Community.

For more information on RAND's International Security and Defense Policy Center, contact the Director, James Dobbins. He can be reached by email at James_Dobbins@rand. org; by phone at 703-413-1100, extension 5134; or by mail at the RAND Corporation, 1200 South Hayes Street, Arlington, VA 22202-5050. More information about RAND is available at www.rand.org.

Contents

Figures and Table

Figures

Table

Summary

The Need to Reorder Priorities

This paper documents an effort to specify requirements for stronger *cognition*—comprehension, reasoning, and decisionmaking—in 21st-century counterinsurgency (COIN). Different from information technology (IT) (e.g., sensors, chat rooms, displays), cognition is what occurs "between the ears" after receiving information. It is as crucial to COIN as physical capabilities, organizational structures, and territorial control, especially against shrewd, distributed insurgents.

Greater attention to cognitive capabilities is dictated by the rise and persistence of a new class of insurgency that combines utopian aims, intense motivation, global connectivity and mobility, extreme violence, and constant adaptation. The foremost example of this is the Islamist-Sunni-Salafist jihad, which aims to overthrow what its adherents see as a corrupt nation-state order in the Muslim world, devised by the West to dominate Islam. Like classical insurgency, the jihad vies for the support of a contested population—in this case, alienated Muslims in both Muslim-majority and Muslim-minority states. Jihad not only aids but also infects local insurgencies with anti-Western venom, religious extremism, and suicide terrorist leanings, making them more vicious and intractable. As we know from Iraq, Afghanistan, and the Levant, such hybrid (global-local) insurgencies are complex, unstable, and harder to comprehend than purely national insurgencies.

The U.S. response to this pattern of insurgency has stressed (1) new bureaucratic layers, e.g., the Department of Homeland Security and the Office of the Director of National Intelligence, that seem to have improved neither analysis nor decisionmaking; (2) increased investment in military platforms, which are of marginal utility against a diffuse and elusive insurgency; and (3) the use of force, which may validate the jihadist argument, producing more jihadis and inspiring new martyrs. What has been missing is a systematic attempt to identify and meet critical analytical, planning, and operational decisionmaking needs for global COIN, exploiting revolutionary progress in information networking. Consequently, U.S. COIN has been as clumsy as the new insurgency has been cunning. Among other benefits, more attention to cognition would improve the cost-effectiveness of U.S. structures, forces, and operations.

The Jihadi Cognitive Challenge

Leaders of the global jihad are charismatic and gifted at strategy and unifying ideology. They skillfully convey a story of relentless American-Christian-Zionist attacks on the global Muslim community (or *ummah*) and Islamic faith, with the violent occupation of Iraq offered as the latest proof. From this comes the call to jihad and martyrdom in *defense* of Islam, which, given the superior military power of the "Crusaders," must include terrorist counterattacks in the West. The ability to tell and sell this story is the energy source of the global Salafist insurgency.

Using this ability, the jihad relies more on intense individual commitment than on advanced weaponry, organizational structure, or territorial control. As Secretary of Defense Donald Rumsfeld has observed, the fact that jihad has no territory to defend makes it harder, not easier, to combat. Even the Salafist idea of a new caliphate, from which Western influence and apostate rulers would be expunged, is more utopian than practical. Jihadis have no practicable scheme or competence for organizing, governing, and defending a nation-state, let alone a vast caliphate. De-territorialization, along with globalization, multiplies jihad's locations, links, cells, and operations, compounding the cognitive challenges of global COIN.

The jihad's ability to generate intense motivation based on individual duty to defend fellow Muslims and Islam is like a resonant cognitive frequency that induces people to commit horrendous acts out of moral conviction. The jihad is able to perpetuate itself by relying on perceived Western injustice and aggression to turn disgruntled Muslims into radical Islamists and then using the story of the West's assault on Islam to recruit radicalized individuals to violence and martyrdom. Understanding this cognitive process is the first step toward breaking it. Preventing Muslims from being radicalized, preventing radicals from choosing violence, and protecting society from violent radicals are different problems requiring different cognitive strategies.

Keeping Muslims from becoming radicals or radicals from becoming terrorists cannot be achieved through a U.S.-led propaganda assault on Islamic fundamentalism any more than it can by reliance on force. Trying to build American domestic support for COIN or to isolate jihadis from other Muslims on ideological or religious grounds may validate the jihadis' story and fulfill their wish for holy war. Where the jihadist argument is weakest is in its theological justification for killing innocents, killing Muslims, and suicide. Provided it is challenged by respected Islamic scholars, as opposed to Western politicians, this weakness can be exploited to undermine potential Muslim public support for jihadis, impede recruitment of new jihadis, and dissuade suicide terror.

While jihad's global aims and reach take it beyond traditional insurgency, it is familiar in the difficulties it poses for the use of deadly force and military occupation. Unlike war between sovereigns, insurgency, local or global, is a contest for the trust and allegiance of a common population. Reliance on force must take into account its likely impact on the sentiment of that population. The classical COIN problem of the ambiguity of force is compounded by the jihadist story that Western attacks on Muslims demand heroic acts of defense by champions of Islam. Killing insurgents may increase their recruits, fanaticism, and violence, making an attrition strategy futile. Moreover, the governing authority and its COIN can fail if the loss of the legitimacy of force puts it on the same level as the insurgents. The answer must be found in smarter COIN, not just at headquarters but spread among the soldiers, police, intelligence agents, and diplomats directly involved with COIN operations.

Cognitive Capabilities for COIN

Smarter COIN demands an improved ability to *understand* the insurgency, to *shape* the conditions in which it vies for public allegiance, and to *act* directly against it.

Understanding jihad requires empirical and innovative research, sensitivity to the psychology of the insurgency and of Muslim populations, vigorous debate in and out of government, and continuous reflection. It also requires advanced analytical tools, an American specialty. Launching a definitive interagency study of jihad would not be fruitful, especially if the findings were negotiated and then frozen for bureaucratic convenience. Against an insurgency as smart as jihad, the effort to understand must be free of the assumptions, constraints, and buzzwords of current policy. It must also be as fluid as the insurgency itself. Analysis should be interdisciplinary and international. Understanding must extend throughout the rank and file of COIN, not held in capitals.

Shaping COIN strategy is largely about enabling the governing power to gain a monopoly in the legitimate use of force in the eyes of the people, even if it cannot gain a monopoly in the capacity for force. Establishing the illegitimacy of jihadist violence is more likely to succeed at acceptable cost than is trying to wipe out all jihadis. The best possibility of delegitimizing jihad lies in its violence against innocents and Muslims, for which there is no basis in accepted Islamic theology. Yet, careless COIN violence, indiscriminant arrests, nonjudicial detention, and cruel interrogation can delegitimize the governing power, validate the jihadist story, legitimize terrorism, and spawn new martyrs. This has been borne out in Iraq, where half of those polled nationwide—and nearly nine out of ten Sunni Arabs—approve of attacks on U.S. forces as a legitimate form of resistance. In contrast, only 1 percent of Iraqis believe that attacks on civilians are justified, whether by jihadis or U.S. forces. The insurgents' strategy of blending in with civilians is intended not only for defense but also to provoke attacks on the contested population. Winning legitimacy under these conditions is fundamentally a cognitive challenge. Effective shaping can reduce the need for force and legitimize force when it is unavoidable.

In COIN *operations*, as in other security operations in the new era, intuition must be integrated with reasoning into a "battle-wise" decisionmaking ability. Intuition alone may not be reliable in unfamiliar situations, whereas reasoning can be aided by networked information. Four cognitive abilities are particularly important in operations: anticipation, opportunism, decision speed, and learning in action. These abilities can be put to good use in operations through *rapid-adaptive* decisionmaking, whereby intuition provides initial direction, creating the opportunity to gather information and reason—all at high speed. With such cognition, COIN can gain an operational *time-information* edge over global insurgency, using time to gain information, using information to gain time, and thus acting in a timely yet informed fashion. COIN does not now enjoy time-information superiority over global insurgency. Rather, it is slow to act when lacking complete information, or else it may produce unwanted results, e.g., civilian deaths, if forced to act in haste. Essential cognitive abilities and decisionmaking methods can be taught.

In COIN, force might weaken an insurgency, strengthen it, or both. With global media and the Internet, violent action against 21st-century insurgency can have such effects globally. Consequently, there is a temptation to rely on, or even tighten, control over COIN by military headquarters or political authorities. Yet, the more diffuse and fluid the insurgency, the less satisfactory centrally controlled COIN will be. Better cognitive abilities must not be concentrated among "the few" at the center but instead spread across "the many" in the field, who must, in turn, have unobstructed access to information, the authority to act, and the chance to collaborate horizontally without deferring to a higher authority. The habit of control must yield to the power of networking.

Finally, COIN must adjust to the reality that the energy source of violent Salafism—the ability to regenerate martyrs and thus perpetuate itself—is not confined to one place, one country, one person. It is increasingly distributed—virtual, not physical. Consequently, this core cannot be destroyed by bombs or commandos alone. It will take cognitive ability, also distributed, to isolate, delegitimize, and extinguish it.

Investment

To improve cognitive capabilities to understand, shape, and operate, a number of investments must be made:

- Cognitive profiles for COIN personnel should be developed.
- The government should gear up to compete vigorously with the private sector to attract people matching these profiles.
- Personnel policies should be tailored to stress COIN cognitive abilities in recruitment, performance evaluation, promotion, assignment, and retention.
- Professional education should address the sorts of problems and choices that arise in COIN analysis, strategy, and operations. Curricula for military, police, and intelligence education should stress analysis and questioning, not rote and groupthink.
- COIN training should be expanded and improved. It should include techniques that integrate intuition with reasoning and foster rapid-adaptive decisionmaking under the stress and uncertainty of COIN conditions.
- COIN training and education should include the study of the process by which ordinary Muslims travel the path to becoming suicide terrorists, including Islamic attitudes, ideals, and grievances, as well as consequences of the use of force.
- Experts on insurgency, Islam, and Muslim populations should be paired with military, police, and intelligence operators.
- Time and space for questioning existing views and for objective research and analysis on jihad should be created within military, policy, and intelligence institutions.

- The personnel departments of military, intelligence, legal, and other national security organizations should be brought into COIN capability-building.
- IT concepts, networks, and applications should be examined critically with a view toward elevating the power and pull of users, along the lines of the Internet-based smart-user revolution.

Along with such investments in cognitive capabilities for COIN is the need for civilian and military institutions involved in COIN to encourage criticism, exploration, and a shift from firepower to brainpower. A smart and dangerous enemy leaves no choice.

Acknowledgments

Several people made important contributions to the thinking, research, and writing that went into this work. Bruce Hoffman and Sara A. Daly provided exacting and helpful reviews. Project team members John Gordon IV, Bruce R. Pirnie, and Martin C. Libicki gave of their time and intellect to challenge and sharpen my analysis. Lesley Warner did a little of everything—actually, a lot of everything—from technical help to research assistance to critical reading for clarity, logic, and substance. I credit all these colleagues for lifting my sights and my effort, though I take sole responsibility for the paper's content and for any errors of fact or reasoning it may contain.

Abbreviations

COIN	counterinsurgency
DoD	U.S. Department of Defense
HUMINT	human intelligence
ISR	intelligence, surveillance, and reconnaissance
IT	information technology
NATO	North Atlantic Treaty Organization
SOF	special operations forces
WMD	weapons of mass destruction

CHAPTER ONE

Introduction: Purpose, Scope, and Definitions

"[C]ounterinsurgency is a thinking man's sport."
—*Colonel Jim Pasquarette, U.S. Army, Iraq, 2006*[1]

This work is an exploration of how to improve cognitive effectiveness in counterinsurgency (COIN). Because these waters are uncharted, the main purpose of this paper is to float ideas for consideration, debate, and further research: initial thoughts, not the last word. At the same time, the basic message is meant to be loud and clear: The United States must give greater attention to the cognitive abilities it needs to combat a persistent and intelligent extremist threat.

Simply stated, cognition in this context means *making sense*—in recognizing and comprehending, in reasoning and problem-solving, in employing intuition, processing facts, and making decisions. In COIN as in other endeavors, effective cognition means more than being knowledgeable, rational, and decisive: It means being wise. That wise strategists and commanders succeed in conflict, all else being equal, is hardly a revelation. But cognitive excellence is especially vital in COIN for one central reason: the ambiguity of force. The relationship between insurgents and contested populations is such that knowing how, when, where, against whom, by whom, and, for that matter, whether to use deadly force is both more difficult and more consequential than in regular warfare.

Appeals are increasing to "fight smarter" against extremist insurgents, a response to frustration over the wars in Iraq and Afghanistan and the persistence of global terrorism:

We will get the better of them only when our thinking is as flexible and innovative as theirs.[2]

Strategy in a global counterinsurgency requires a new level of thinking.[3]

[We] need the education, the insight, and the appreciation of the human terrain to develop COIN campaigns.[4]

---

[1] Quoted in Ignatius (2006).

[2] Benjamin and Simon (2006).

[3] Barno (2006, p. 27).

[4] Celeski (2005).

A successful global COIN [requires] the capacity to take decisive yet thoughtful action against terrorists and/or insurgents in uncertain situations.[5]

While such sentiments are surely right, they will not actually produce smarter COIN, any more than exhorting a classroom of students to think harder will improve their test scores. In COIN, as in the schoolhouse, it takes homework to get smarter—purposeful policies, programs, and investments based on disciplined analysis of the role and requirements of cognition. This paper is meant to go beyond the plea to fight smarter by examining *how* to do so.

Information technology (IT) provides an unprecedented opportunity to improve cognition in COIN, but no more than an opportunity. Thanks to data networking, plentiful information is now available to support operations of all sorts, including COIN.[6] The ability to make sense of and use of this information is as crucial as any mechanized or electronic COIN capability, especially against insurgents who are distributed, shrewd, elusive, and fanatical. Efforts by the United States and its security partners to enhance cognitive capabilities for COIN will require no less analytical rigor, no less care in setting requirements, no less focus in making investments than more tangible capabilities do. For this reason, the larger RAND COIN study of which this paper is a part is giving as much attention to the cognitive layer of COIN capabilities as it is to the information, physical, structural, and geographic layers.

The first step is to distinguish between the technology that facilitates the exchange of information and the mental abilities that use information to reason and make decisions. All too often, discussion of sense-making wanders into the realm of IT gadgetry, where our comfort level is higher than it is in "thinking about thinking." Aiding cognition by developing and applying technology is different from improving it by developing and applying brainpower. So-called "information superiority" offered by advanced sensors, global data networks, and user-friendly displays is not the same as, and does not ensure, superior thinking. Cognitive excellence requires enhancements in key mental abilities and thus in the recruitment, retention, preparation, assignment, and empowerment of the soldiers, intelligence agents, diplomats, and analysts engaged in COIN. In sum, this paper is about how minds, not machines, perform.

Cognitive excellence is not simply a matter of having smart commanders. Gone are the days when brilliance in warfare could or had to be concentrated in a few decisionmakers at the top. Insurgencies are *complex dynamic systems*, with many political, military, and psychological "moving parts" and feedback circuits. Direct local contact with such systems—with insurgents and contested populations—is needed to sense what is happening and to respond intelligently.

Yet, tactical judgments can have widespread and enduring strategic effects. A paradox of counterinsurgency is that the use of force might weaken an insurgency, strengthen it, or both. In countering *global* insurgency (addressed later in this chapter), the use of force can have effects, intended or not, virtually anywhere in the world. Violence against civilians or cruel treatment of detainees in Iraq can cause a violent reaction from Indonesia to Morocco

---

[5]   Ongoing, unpublished RAND research on countering terrorism and insurgency.

[6]   A companion RAND study will take up the question of how to apply IT more effectively in COIN.

and furor among Europe's Muslims, especially if communicated via insurgency Internet links, broadcast through global media, or stirred into existing animosities.

Consequently, military headquarters and political authorities are inclined to rely on and even to tighten central control over COIN, using the same IT that otherwise allows control to be *de*centralized.[7] The need for the "left hand" and "right hand" to work in tandem is critical in COIN and reinforces the urge for central control. Yet, the more diffuse, complex, and fluid the insurgency, the less responsive and successful centrally controlled COIN will be.[8] The more distributed the insurgency, the more crucial it is to respond with distributed COIN, exploiting the advantages of time, agility, and reach offered by networking.[9] In the face of global insurgency, COIN must be both intelligent and distributed—a tall order.

Distributed information is most potent when decisionmaking is also distributed. This suggests a need to improve reasoning and problem-solving abilities not just for "the few" at the center but also for "the many" in the field, be they soldiers, intelligence agents, police, diplomats, or aid workers.[10] Moreover, "the many" must have the authority to decide and act, as well as the opportunity to collaborate with one another without having to defer to a higher command; otherwise, only a fraction of the cognitive capacity of the entire COIN effort can be mobilized. This need to decentralize authority and foster horizontal collaboration has major implications for how to develop and use cognitive capabilities in COIN.

Thus, in 21st-century COIN, habits of tight, central control must yield to the power available through the networking of informed and intelligent actors, each authorized to act, react, and adapt, yet all informed by shared purpose and strategy. This is all the more important when faced with an insurgency that is dispersed, complex, and adaptive, as is the one of greatest current concern to the United States. In turn, as cognitive abilities are improved throughout the ranks of COIN, political and military leaders must and can concentrate on strategic reasoning and decisionmaking. The mental challenge to political-military leadership in today's COIN is in creating unity of effort among eclectic elements without micromanaging them. This way, COIN can be at once intelligent, decentralized, *and* integrated, as it must be against the likes of al Qaeda.

With this notion as a backdrop, this paper offers ideas for gaining cognitive advantage in countering a new, *globally distributed* class of insurgency characterized by supranational aims, ideological or religious fanaticism, transnational connectivity and mobility, a loose- and flat-networked cellular structure, adaptability, the capacity for regeneration, and a preference for shocking violence. Networking allows this class of insurgency to be at once global and local,

---

[7] Kilcullen (2005).

[8] The model of a federated insurgency enabled by networking, the basis for much of the analysis in this paper, is borrowed from ongoing, unpublished research at RAND.

[9] Ongoing, unpublished RAND research on future insurgency threats.

[10] In theory and increasingly in reality, those on the periphery of a network can have all relevant information available anywhere on the network. In addition, they have information about their immediate circumstances that is not on the network; this is often called "latent knowledge." This combination means that network nodes may have more relevant data than do network hubs, which in turn places a premium on giving them both the authority to act and the cognitive abilities to act wisely. (See Gompert, Lachow, and Perkins, 2005.)

making it all the harder to understand. COIN, in response, must address the global and the local, the core and the periphery, the hub and the nodes, the whole and the parts. Such a monumental challenge will require distributed cognitive excellence.

The foremost example of global insurgency, if not the first full-fledged case, is the Islamist-Sunni-Salafist (hereafter simply *Salafist*) jihad that rages from Southeast Asia to northwest Iraq to northern Africa to central London.[11] A RAND research team has concluded that the jihad "can and should be viewed as the first truly global insurgency."[12] Whether this is first-of-a-class or one-of-a-kind is unclear. As two British colleagues on this project state, "The Muslim dimension is so overwhelming it raises a question of whether global insurgency is a generic phenomenon in the evolution of insurgency or a uniquely Muslim phenomenon which no other archipelago of populations could emerge to reproduce."[13]

To label this pattern of violence *insurgency* is not to suggest that it fits neatly into the conventional definition of insurgency as a violent, popular-based opposition movement aimed at seizing control of a nation-state. Rather, it represents a major development in the evolution of insurgency, owing above all to the globalization of both means and ends. It also reflects the fact that Muslims, more than persons of other beliefs, identify with their religious community regardless, or instead, of nationality, especially now that the Internet and global media spread information throughout the global Muslim population.

How can we call widespread Islamist terrorism insurgency if its goal is different from and larger than gaining control of a nation-state? Let's not forget that the nation-state is a European invention, the enduring primacy of which is assumed by Westerners; competitively, it has served the West well and has been appliquéd by the West on much of the rest of the globe, including the Muslim world. On the whole, the nation-state has been unhelpful and unkind to Muslims, and today it signifies rule by illegitimate and apostate regimes in bed with the West. As identification with a nation-state wears thin among Muslim populations, identification with Islam deepens. In turn, the nation-state may become less hospitable to conspicuously practicing Muslims, reinforcing their orientation toward religious instead of national identity. One can understand why Muslims, especially Islamists, could have greater allegiance to their worldwide religious community than to any nation-state, as well as why their concerns and ambitions are not aligned with the nation-state boundaries they consider artificial. Jihadist theoreticians see the Muslim community as an alternative or successor to "the prevailing paradigm of international structures and state-to-state interaction."[14]

The violent global Salafist insurgency aims not so much to rule this or that nation-state as to overturn the existing Western-dominated nation-state order, at least within the Muslim-

---

[11] One can imagine other possible widely distributed insurgencies that could threaten U.S. security interests: a new, networked, violent surge of leftist anti-American or antiglobalization sentiment throughout Latin America; neo-Maoist rebellion against monarchic or oligarchic regimes in Asia and elsewhere. While these may seem unlikely to rise to the significance of global jihad, it is important to keep in mind both the operational capabilities and the motivational potency that could come with increased global connectivity and mobility.

[12] Ongoing, unpublished RAND research on future insurgency threats.

[13] Mackinlay and Al-Baddawy (forthcoming).

[14] Mackinlay and Al-Baddawy (forthcoming).

majority parts of the world. To that end, it uses a mix of terror, asymmetric warfare, propaganda, and popular legitimacy akin to that of traditional insurgency. The contested population in this insurgency is a Muslim community that has become detached from its nation-states' frame of reference and is acquiring its own personality, aided by global connectivity. Jihadis see themselves, and are widely seen, as this community's champions and defenders.

Whatever we call it, do not expect the fighters and terrorists of the Salafist jihad to confine themselves to traditional insurgent tactics, which are typically geared toward winning the widest possible popular sympathy as a way of gaining national political control. Likewise, calling jihad *insurgency* does not signify that the means and methods of traditional COIN are entirely appropriate. If only because of its global diffusion, the Salafist insurgency requires different countermeasures: among them, as this paper will argue, is a greater reliance on *distributed cognitive excellence*. While expert opinion might differ on whether the nomenclature of insurgency and COIN is apt in this case, it is surely better than that of terrorism and counterterrorism, which describes only a weapon of choice.

By the same token, to call this extremist violence *jihad* is not to deny nor denigrate the Muslim concept of inner (nonviolent) struggle as a means to become a better person. However, jihad can also mean *holy war,* of the most violent sort, against a Western-dominated international order that purportedly threatens Islam. The words of a standard Saudi Arabian 12th-grade textbook hardly suggest a quest for individual betterment: "Jihad in the path of God—which consists of battling against unbelief, oppression, injustice, and those who perpetrate it—is the summit of Islam. This religion arose through jihad and through jihad was its banner raised high."[15] Jihad is used by the orchestrators of the modern holy war with the knowledge that it will resonate with many Muslims as a call to duty. In their original 1998 fatwa launching worldwide jihad, Osama bin Laden and Ayman al-Zawahiri were clear: "We . . . call on every Muslim who believes in God and wishes to be rewarded to comply with God's order to kill the Americans."[16]

Thus, this paper will treat the self-proclaimed *jihad* as a new anti-Westphalian kind of *insurgency,* one that is global in its aims and reach, while recognizing that these expressions have differing interpretations and should not, by themselves, dictate particular counterstrategies.[17] Whatever the terminology, the key is to cognize the phenomenon *for what it is* and then to blend useful experience with innovative ways of countering it.[18]

In the taxonomy of the larger RAND COIN study of which this is a part, the ideas of this paper apply to Class IV (global-diffuse) insurgency and Class III (global-local) insurgency.

---

[15] Shea (2006).

[16] "Al Qaeda's Fatwa" (English translation, 1998).

[17] The Peace of Westphalia of 1648 established the primacy and inviolability of sovereign nation-states following the Thirty Years' War, which wracked Europe with religious violence. This treaty signified the beginning of the era in which sovereigns are bound to respect one another. Anti-Westphalian forces are those that reject this principle of international order and regard many if not all nation-states as increasingly artificial.

[18] Al Qaeda, its affiliates, and its imitators are being redefined by some in research and policy circles not as terrorist organizations but instead as insurgencies, in the general sense of being movements that seek to overthrow the prevailing order through subversion, armed conflict, and terrorism. Among the sources that have identified jihad as a global insurgency are David J. Kilcullen, John Mackinlay, and prior RAND research. (See Kilcullen, 2005; Mackinlay, 2005.)

The other two classes are local-national insurgency (Class I) and local insurgency with international support (Class II). Because of their global dimension, the cognitive demands of Class III and IV insurgencies deserve special attention. At the same time, cognitive excellence is important in countering traditional classes of insurgency (Classes I and II). Even before al Qaeda, the record of COIN is not so stellar—Vietnam and Algeria come to mind—as to suggest that past modes of thinking have been adequate for analysis, strategy, or action.

In considering how to gain a cognitive advantage in COIN, it is helpful to follow an analytical trail that begins with understanding the insurgents and the problems they pose, then identifies capabilities needed to counter them, and ultimately points to specific investments and policies to develop and use those capabilities. In following this trail, this paper will show how to derive investments from problems posed—a method used in the larger RAND study.

Structurally, the paper continues, in Chapter Two, by clarifying what is meant by cognitive capabilities for COIN and why they are so relevant to countering the global Salafist jihad. It then lays out in Chapter Three the general case for reordering priorities among U.S. capabilities in this struggle. Chapter Four takes an in-depth look at the cognitive challenges posed by global jihad. From this, the challenge to close the cognitive gap for COIN is presented in Chapter Five, and specific cognitive requirements of global COIN, detailed in Chapter Six, are established. Chapter Seven presents a description of the capabilities to meet those requirements. The paper concludes in Chapter Eight with ideas concerning potential investments to create better capabilities and institutional reforms to give increased attention and improved direction to cognition in COIN.

The idea that good understanding, reasoning, and decisionmaking have a vital role in COIN is not new, begging the question of why the United States is not better at these cognitive aspects.[19] After all, it seems obvious that success in any conflict entangled in the anger and aspirations of a population requires more brainpower than firepower. Obvious or not, the importance of cognitive effectiveness seems to be forgotten in practice. Research *prior* to the Vietnam War came to the following conclusion: "If the U.S. is to work successfully through a local people, it is essential that an understanding concerning how that society functions be developed on the part of the [COIN] personnel involved, to enable them to *anticipate correctly the results of the actions they plan to take*."[20] Within a few years of that prescription, U.S. armed forces were using napalm against South Vietnamese. Theorizing about the need for cognitive excellence in COIN does no good if it is not applied. For this reason, this paper will offer concrete, if preliminary, suggestions for application.

The analysis that follows does not address the matter of the relative importance of the Salafist jihad in American security strategy and national security priorities. To be clear, the author considers this insurgency to be dangerous, countering it to be difficult, and success to be important, though not at any cost of American lives, resources, rights, and ideals.

---

[19] One explanation for why the United States is not better at the understanding, reasoning, and decisionmaking components of successful COIN comes from Eliot Cohen et al.: "After Vietnam, the U.S. Army reacted to the threat of irregular warfare chiefly by saying 'never again.' The study of counterguerilla and COIN operations was leached from the various military college curricula" (Cohen et al., 2006, p. 53).

[20] Sorenson and Pack (1964, p. 2); emphasis added.

CHAPTER TWO

The Mind as Central Front

Increased emphasis on cognitive effectiveness in analysis, strategy, and operations vis-à-vis global jihad is consistent with a broader shift of emphasis among the factors of warfare from the mechanical domain to the informational and, beyond that, the cognitive.[1] This shift is the product of several effects of the dual information and geopolitical revolutions of the last several decades: accessible network infrastructure, fluid international conditions, irregular and transnational threats, and unfamiliar operational circumstances. As warfare becomes more distributed, and more bewildering, the value of being able to make sense and use of networked information "at the edge" of warfighting structures grows.[2] Yet, analysis of cognitive requirements and how to meet them has lagged. Although some U.S. Department of Defense (DoD) documents mention in general terms a need for improvement in the "cognitive domain," there is no program to do so for COIN or otherwise.[3]

It is, as mentioned, especially critical to strengthen cognitive capabilities to counter a complex, distributed, and mutating global insurgency that excels at using information. The Salafist jihad, which includes al Qaeda and other groups, local and global, preaches and practices holy war against "the West," Christians, Jews, and apostate Muslims.[4] In theory, it is drawn by the vision of a puritanical pan-Muslim caliphate out of which Western influence and apostate regimes are to be cast, in which Muslims are to live and worship safely, and from which a final assault against infidels is to be mounted. In fact, the jihadist fire is stoked by a claim that Islam and Muslims are under American and Zionist attack and are left with no choice but to *counterattack.*

Such ideas are not explicitly called for by the Koran or other Islamic scriptures. Rather, Salafist extremists interpret religious texts—*hadiths* and *suras*—along such lines to convince disaffected Muslims of the righteousnesss of violence in the name of Allah and in defense of

---

[1] The theory being that as more information becomes available through networking, those with an advantage in making sense and use of the information will, all else being equal, have a competitive or operational advantage.

[2] Alberts and Hayes (2003); Gompert, Lachow, and Perkins (2005).

[3] See, for example, Director, Office of Force Transformation, Office of the Secretary of Defense (2003).

[4] There are differences among important al Qaeda figures on the permissibility of killing Muslims, with Osama bin Laden and al-Zawahiri generally opposed and al-Zarqawi unhesitant.

Islam.[5] That they are able to generate streams of religious warriors without an authoritative religious basis attests to the intellectual ability of jihadist strategists.

At the heart of their ability is not theological scholarship but instead a message that Muslims are being persecuted for their religion by a militarily powerful, religiously motivated Christian-Jewish alliance. While the operating mode of global jihad has been one of bold offense, the frame of mind is one of desperate *defense*. This accounts for the ability of jihadist intellectuals to produce not only militants but also martyrs throughout the global Muslim community. Casting global holy war as desperately defensive can make suicide terrorism a compulsory individual duty for some.

Again, as al Qaeda and its affiliates and imitators see it, the political order that is to be counterattacked is not just the regime of this or that nation-state but rather a Western-designed, U.S.-dominated international order that is hostile to Islam and harmful to Muslims. Both post- and pre-Westphalian—it was, after all, transnational religious war that prompted European sovereigns to agree in 1648 to respect one another thereafter—violent Salafism regards modern nation-states not as entities to covet but as units of an order they abhor.

This hostile and illegitimate order includes nation-states with Muslim majorities. There is no hint of national patriotism in the words or actions of most jihadist leaders.[6] On the contrary, a premise of the jihad is that the Muslim community has been balkanized to facilitate Western dominance. According to bin Laden, "[I]t is essential to hit the main enemy who divided the Ummah [the Muslim community] into small and little countries and pushed it, for the last few decades, into a state of confusion."[7] Salafist extremism is diametrically opposed to modern nationalism, which has largely failed the Arab world. True jihadis in Iraq are not interested in gaining control of the country but in destroying it as a nation-state.

Moreover, jihadis locate wherever they can and must to defend the Muslim community and to strike against its attackers: Egyptians in Pakistan, Pakistanis in the United Kingdom, Jordanians in Iraq, Bengalis in Canada, Yemenis in Europe, Chechens in Bosnia, Saudis in New York. Statelessness, complexity, and long tentacles make global jihad all the more confounding, thus underscoring the need to improve the ability to comprehend it and act wisely against it.

As Iraq has shown, the supranational Salafist jihad can inflame and exploit subnational insurgencies to its advantage, as is the case with once-privileged Iraqi Sunnis enraged by U.S. occupation and opposed to the country's new political order. When global insurgency attaches itself to local insurgency, the global one may not only aid the local one but also infuse it with jihadist zeal and terrorist methods. Even if there are differences in goals or means between globalized jihadis and local insurgents that could be exploited, as there may now be in Iraq, the former can impart to the latter the mindset to commit unrestrained violence and to sneer

---

[5] The lives of Mohammed and his contemporary followers were, of course, filled with armed conflict both against and by them.

[6] Pakistan seems to be an exception, which could be explained by the fact that it was a Muslim state by conception. The mix of nationalism and religious fundamentalism is also evident in Shiite Iran.

[7] Bin Laden interview in Pape (2005, p. 52); bracketed text in original.

at negotiation. As one expert puts it, "The blending of terrorism with . . . insurgents manifests itself in an exceedingly dangerous form."[8]

The Sunni insurgency in Iraq has become both more vicious and more resilient since it began shifting to a religious footing in early 2004. It is a mistake to equate jihad with foreign fighters, as growing numbers of Iraqis have turned, or returned, to Islamic extremism. Foreigners are not the primary agents in drawing Sunni insurgents to Salafism: Most are swayed by communications from "global" Salafis (e.g., al Qaeda) or by radicalized Iraqi-Sunni clerics. Many insurgent groups now blend Salafist-extremist ideology (religious fundamentalism) and methods (suicide killings) with Sunni political demands.[9] The secular Ba'athism that spawned the Sunni insurgency as its first impetus and its first fighters has largely given way to, or been swallowed up by, radical religious forces, Iraqi or foreign. Ironically, the Salafism that Saddam's elites dreaded has given the insurgency new life.

Even without foreign jihadis, the infection of local insurgencies with the ideology of global holy war makes them more deadly and implacable. Disgruntled Sunnis might abandon insurgency if they gain more representation in the Iraqi government; Iraqi Salafist jihadis have a very different aim and will not be won over or bought off by political power sharing. While this could result in a split and weakening of the Sunni insurgency, it also implies that at least some faction will fight on regardless of political offers or deals to share power.

We see that the extreme violence of those who reject the very idea of a pluralistic Iraq destroys the prospect of negotiations and provokes Shiite militants to strike back. Instead of the insurgency being quieted by the process of political inclusion, we see it bringing on a sectarian war, precisely what the jihadists have in mind.

A continent away, in Thailand, what was a low-grade separatist movement in the Muslim Patani province is now proclaimed as a jihad by directive of God, meant to kill all who are out to destroy Islam, including Muslims who betray Islamic principles.[10] The fingerprints of Salafist agency are unmistakable: The Patani insurgents' ideological handbook is written in Arabic as well as the local language.

The brains of global jihad are ingenious, the voices persuasive. The "value" that the cognitive core adds to insurgent capabilities and operations lies mainly in its strategic messaging, with operational planning, logistics, weapon-building, finance, and execution left to lesser nodes in the network.[11] If cognition is a core competency of the jihad, it should be a core competency of COIN as well. Classical COIN teaches that trying to crush intelligent insurgencies with brute force usually fails. And fail it will against a global insurgency whose resonance with militants depends on the argument that Muslims are targets of brute force and must fight back. Jihadist organizations count on the United State to use force—the more excessive, massive, and publicized, the better. They seek to cause U.S. forces to overreact.

---

[8] Celeski (2005).

[9] International Crisis Group (2006a).

[10] Moore (2006).

[11] Analysis of the roles of cores, hubs, and peripheral nodes in jihadist networks is drawn from an ongoing, unpublished RAND study on future insurgency threats.

Against an adversary that feeds on the force of its adversary, off-the-shelf models of insurgency and COIN must be applied with great caution.[12] The jihad's increasingly distributed cellular form and its integration with larger populations further reduce the utility of military force and territorial control as a counterstrategy. As David Kilcullen, a leading Australian analyst now serving in the U.S. Department of State, argues, it is correct to regard global jihad as an insurgency but wrong to apply the "standard model" of COIN to try to get the better of it: "[Whereas] classical counterinsurgency seeks to deny enemy sanctuaries, prevent infiltration . . . and isolate insurgents from support, . . . global insurgency has limited vulnerability to many of these measures, because of the phenomenon of . . . under-administered areas."[13] Whenever the utility of experience-based models is in doubt, in COIN or otherwise, fresh thinking and objective reasoning based on new data are imperative.

The first cognitive task is to "know the enemy," in both its recognizable and unrecognizable aspects. In some ways, global jihad resembles prior classes of insurgencies. It has

- an interest in legitimizing its actions and in delegitimizing the actions and forces of the governing order
- operational dependence on popular support
- a practice of avoidance of force-on-force combat
- a greater reliance on patience and motivation than does the adversary
- a history of celebration and exploitation of martyrdom.

Yet, in other respects jihad is unfamiliar. There is

- disinterest in territorial control
- an absence of a practical political agenda[14]
- a willingness and ability to join local movements anywhere (e.g., Palestinians, Sunni Iraqis, separatists from the Caucasus to Southeast Asia, alienated Muslims in the West).[15]
- a disinclination to negotiate
- global mobility and connectivity
- individual rather than collective duty

---

[12] Herbert Simon, the noted economist, observed in 1950 that the ability of the mind to comprehend complex, dynamic reality was so limited that humans depend on mental models, which are not only simpler than reality but may predispose us toward a flawed, if familiar, understanding of and solution to problems. This is an observation worth heeding as we contemplate global-diffuse insurgencies and how to counter them.

[13] Kilcullen (2005, p. 615).

[14] Some groups that are drawn toward or exploited by global jihad have such agendas, and the jihadist leadership may identify with and support them, at least fleetingly. Examples include Iraq, Chechnya, and Kashmiri insurgents, and various separatist or extremist groups in Southeast Asia.

[15] Whether local movements are prepared to team with the global Salafist movement is, of course, a different matter. The ultimate goal of Hamas is a homeland of Palestinians, not assimilation into some grand caliphate. At the same time, Hamas has embraced religious as well as political agendas and may associate itself with common Islamist themes at least to gain outside support and motivate its followers.

- a preference for violence that maximizes shock, awe, and casualties, and an indifference toward public revulsion.

These differences between classical and global insurgency are not random. True, al Qaeda's evolution is partly in response to the opportunities and dangers of its environment, including the demonstrated ability of U.S. forces to obliterate large and known insurgent concentrations. But there is also intelligent design at work. The minds of jihad appreciate the potential for a new, diffuse form of insurgency that can simultaneously utilize and attack globalization, elude the ability to understand and react, and use information as a weapon. The importance of the cognitive domain is also well understood by the jihad's brain trust. Bin Laden is reported to have said well before 9/11 that information is "90 percent of battle preparation."[16] A defining strength of this insurgency is its keen awareness of its milieu, of the psyche of its prospective recruits, and of the vulnerabilities of its enemies.

This strategic sophistication is evident in the ideas and influence of Mustafa Setmariam Nasar (captured in Pakistan in 2005), who is described as the "best theoretician among the jihadis."[17] His widely distributed strategy, *The Call for a Global Resistance,* and other papers outline a plan for "a revolutionary jihad for the sake of Allah." The plan spells out the doctrine of decentralized global jihad, based on drawing individuals and small groups worldwide into a common ideology. These ideas transcend traditional insurgency and even the original al Qaeda.[18] In addition to their intrinsic significance, they reveal the capacity of the jihad to learn and thus to change and perpetuate. Such qualities in global insurgency raise first-order questions about U.S. COIN priorities.

---

[16] Statement from a captured letter by Osama bin Laden to Mullah Muhammad Omar. (See bin Laden, undated, for full text of letter with alternative translation.)

[17] Brynjar Lia, Norwegian counterterrorism researcher, quoted in Whitlock (2006).

[18] Whitlock (2006).

CHAPTER THREE

Reordering COIN Priorities

What makes the global jihad so difficult and dangerous is its ability to commandeer globalization, religious devotion, and Muslims' sense of community for violent purposes. This ability relies on a story that Muslims are under attack. When the United States and its allies conduct attacks on Muslims, whether for COIN or other reasons, the story is reinforced and the jihad is reinvigorated. The U.S. invasion and occupation of Iraq is used to refresh the story and to impose on Muslims a new and more compelling personal duty to defend the community. Given the efficacy of suicide terrorism, it is unnecessary to convince large communities of jihadis to accept this duty.

This is an insurgency that draws strength from the strength used against it. The more fragmented, dispersed, and embedded global jihad becomes, the harder it becomes to use force against it without confirming the jihadist story. Dependence on military power, a high priority in U.S. COIN since 9/11, is unlikely to succeed against jihad, and could even help an adversary with this logic and the cognitive and communications skills to project it. U.S. COIN must place a higher priority on cognitive capabilities if it is to weaken the ability of jihad to regenerate itself by recruiting fresh martyrs to defend Islam. This must translate into a high priority on sound analysis and decisions in all key aspects of COIN: understanding, shaping the conditions of, and acting against this insurgency.

The need to understand the cognitive strengths and strategies of insurgencies, and to invest in cognitive effectiveness for COIN, did not appear suddenly with global jihad. This aspect of COIN has rarely received sufficient attention, which helps to explain the unimpressive success rate. During the Vietnam War, U.S. strategy emphasized a combination of firepower, political ideology, and economic aid at the expense of understanding the strength of Vietnamese nationalism, the appeal of unification, and the genius of North Vietnamese military leadership.[1] Moreover, the refusal or inability of the U.S. government to be objective and forthright about that conflict, even with itself, undermined sound reasoning and decisionmaking. Successful COIN is hard enough when its planners and practitioners are totally objective. When they are not, it is impossible.

Recognition of the centrality of cognitive performance in insurgency and COIN is also a reminder of the limits of organizational "solutions." Confidence in structuring for success is a product of the United States' corporate mentality and its 20th-century success in organiz-

---

[1] Ongoing, unpublished RAND research on air power in the new counterinsurgency era.

ing to win industrial-territorial war, especially World War II and the Cold War. Already, it is apparent that restructuring to counter global insurgency is at best insufficient and at worst a distraction. There is no denying that after 9/11, U.S. homeland security needed to be organized for better focus on global counterinsurgency and that U.S. intelligence agencies needed to be connected for better information sharing. However, when countering a dynamic threat, faith in structure is faith misplaced.

U.S. military and intelligence establishments have been conditioned by decades of dealing with an enemy far less flexible, and arguably less intelligent, than global jihad. In the 1970s and 1980s, the Soviet system was even slower to adjust than the United States, and it paid the price by being unable to keep up with changes in the world and in strategic competition caused by the information revolution. With the United States racing ahead of the Soviet Union in technological and economic fields, the U.S. defense and intelligence bureaucracies could afford at the time to be nearly as slow to adapt as the Kremlin.

If the Soviet Union was a casualty of the information revolution, the current global jihad is one of its children. The jihad moves and morphs at the pace of markets, much faster than the U.S security apparatus. It has changed radically in the five years it has taken the U.S. government to restructure homeland security and intelligence based on the threat as it was in 2001. And the jihad will keep changing even as post-9/11 U.S. security structures continue ironing out their "wrinkles" and settling into new routines. Bureaucracies gravitate toward equilibrium. Not so global jihad, which craves instability. Insurgency changes continuously as a function of its environment, while COIN changes only when its commanders can no longer ignore the need to do so.[2]

Whatever else it achieves, reorganization does not predictably yield better analysis and operational decisionmaking, which depend on how and how well people think rather than how their bureaus are organized. Insofar as U.S. reorganization for global COIN adds bureaucratic tiers, such as the Office of the Director of National Intelligence and the Department of Homeland Security, its contribution to clear thinking and creative problem-solving is questionable. The U.S. governmental need to centralize and have someone "in charge" is the opposite of the increasingly loose and splintered structure of jihad. Civilian and military bureaucracies—the former with their processes and the latter with their manuals—are antithetical to rapid learning from one's own and the enemy's mistakes, and thus are no answer to jihad's adaptability. The U.S. intelligence establishment does not foster the free and nonlinear thinking that is needed to fathom the unfamiliar and changing phenomena associated with global insurgency.

Spending patterns are also revealing. To wage its "long war" against global jihad, the U.S. government continues to increase spending on conventional military forces (by another 7 percent for 2007). An increase of roughly $150 billion in annual DoD spending since 2001 dwarfs growth for the same period in spending on all other federal policy arms critical to counterterrorism combined (e.g., the Departments of Justice, State, and Homeland Security)

---

[2] Mackinlay and Al-Baddawy (forthcoming).

by a margin of five to one.[3] This growth is comprised of operating costs (for Afghanistan and Iraq, on top of ordinary expenses) and investment in military equipment. Most existing and proposed programs to build aircraft, ships, and combat vehicles are justified to Congress and the public as necessary for the "global war on terrorism."[4] Just how useful all this expensive hardware is in global COIN is a matter that should be examined objectively: Some of it could have value; much of it has little.

Even smarter weapons and smarter platforms to carry them cannot be the primary instruments in outsmarting a diffuse and mobile insurgency that can exist and act practically anywhere, including within crowded population centers into which even the smartest weapons cannot be fired. Although precision standoff weapons and unmanned aerial vehicles can be used to take out key jihadis on occasion, they do not help against insurgents hidden in Muslim communities. Images of smoldering rubble are used to prove the ruthlessness of U.S. war on Muslims.

Of all its military capabilities, DoD has at last officially recognized the exceptional value of special operations forces (SOF) in counterterrorism and global COIN. (Until this year, the SOF share of the DoD budget had actually declined since 2001 and is still less than 2 percent.) SOF are as noted for their cognitive ability as they are for their fighting ability.[5] In addition to SOF, DoD increasingly understands the importance of intelligence, surveillance, reconnaissance, command and control in COIN.[6] On the whole, though, the military has been slow, or reluctant, to rethink the utility in COIN of much of its conventional warfighting capability. In general, if COIN capabilities are thought of as three bins—understand, shape, and attack—the U.S. government continues to shovel most of its resources into the third.

American enchantment with technology to achieve security should also be questioned. The United States excels in information networking, detection, and precision. Drawing on and exploiting this strength certainly should be stressed in global COIN.[7] At the same time, two of the chief lessons of the information revolution are (1) that IT spreads rapidly and is easy to use and (2) that IT does not guarantee better results but instead liberates and enables humans to do what they do best: reason and decide. U.S. COIN has no monopoly in access to and sharing of information, and whichever side makes better sense and use of it will have operational and strategic advantages. IT does not reduce but rather increases the importance of enhancing cognitive capabilities in COIN.

In sum, global COIN will not succeed against global insurgency if it relies exclusively on organizational, physical, and IT capabilities; territorial control; and the use of force. Against

---

[3] In fact, it is those civilian agencies that, in conjunction with friendly governments around the world, have neutralized the most al Qaeda operatives and foiled the most terrorist threats since the fall of the Taliban in late 2001.

[4] The Joint Chiefs of Staff just announced that Trident submarine–launched ballistic missiles, the workhorse of the U.S. intercontinental strategic arsenal, could be used to combat terrorism (Rutz, 2006).

[5] The Department of Defense Quadrennial Defense Review (DoD, 2006) places much greater stress on SOF, and the fiscal year 2007 budget reflects this in the form of increasing resources for SOF by roughly 20 percent.

[6] This is evident in a speech by Under Secretary of Defense for Policy Eric Edelman on March 30, 2006, which stressed information, intelligence, and awareness (see Garamone, 2006).

[7] A parallel study of needed U.S. information capabilities has been undertaken as part of RAND's COIN study.

an adversary whose best weapon is brainpower, the United States will need to decide how to improve and engage more brainpower of its own. Compared to the nation's commitment of neurons to other large endeavors (e.g., writing search programs and mapping genomes) countering global jihad looks like a low priority. One reason for this disparity is that financial returns of private enterprise attract, motivate, and reward genius better than government can, including for COIN. Short of a national call to arms on the scale of World War II, the government will have to be resourceful in improving and using the brainpower available for countering jihad.

Honing cognitive capabilities for global COIN would also improve the cost-effectiveness of structural, technological, and physical capabilities, which are currently a heavy burden on the U.S. federal budget and economy. Some $400 billion have been spent trying to counter jihad in Iraq and Afghanistan, with mixed results in those countries and without stemming the wider insurgency. Greater stress on effective analysis could make *all* investments in COIN go further and return more. Yet there is no known government-wide effort to analyze where to invest its "next dollar" for greatest effect in countering global jihad.

As noted, a strategy to enhance cognitive capabilities in global COIN will mainly take the form of practical policy measures and investments in *people*: recruitment, retention, development, training, education, assignment, and command and control in U.S. diplomatic, development, defense, intelligence, and research establishments.[8] The personnel shops of government must be brought into the effort and guided strategically. In danger of being outsmarted, the United States needs to organize and continuously tune better analytical, strategic, and decisionmaking abilities than it has to date in countering global jihad.

Compare the strategy and priorities of the U.S. government since the globalization of insurgency (say, 2000) with those of Google, the reigning leader of Internet competition during the same period. Google knows that its strategic edge and market success depend above all on attracting, motivating, and utilizing human talent. It seeks to dominate the labor market for the most capable and innovative software engineers in the world.[9] Google's strategy, pure and simple, is to out-think the competition, and its rise is attributable to doing just that. In contrast, the U.S. government, with its emphasis on structures (Department of Homeland Security, Office of the Director of National Intelligence), conventional military capabilities (planes and ships), and territorial control (Afghanistan and Iraq), has shown no corresponding commitment to countering the jihad by assembling and using exceptional national brainpower.

There are instructive precedents in U.S. history. World War II was as much about mustering American brainpower as it was about harnessing industrial power. The Manhattan Project, often cited as a model of how to solve the most daunting puzzles, was largely a matter of herding an unruly bunch of scientists toward a single goal, despite differences in their motivations and their opposition to being structured and constrained. The key to the Manhattan Project

---

[8]   Such an emphasis is articulated in ongoing, unpublished RAND research on countering terrorism and insurgency, which calls for "retaining, recruiting, and developing people with appropriate language and intercultural communication skills, expertise in training and executing military tasks, and a detailed understanding of interagency and coalition operations."

[9]   Google hires one out of every 1,000 applicants, yet it hires the majority of the best software engineers available.

was the skill of J. Robert Oppenheimer in energizing and channeling the thinking of the scientists while shielding them from government bureaucracy.[10] Had the War Department had its way in managing that brainpower, the project would probably not have borne fruit when it did.

Or consider the American response to the Soviet Sputnik challenge of 1957: It was less about rocket thrust than about scientific excellence, culminating in the Apollo missions to the Moon. The strategic shock and soul-searching in the aftermath of Sputnik led to a commitment to improve and harness national education. No such effort to identify and meet critical analytical, planning, and decisionmaking needs has occurred since 9/11. While 20th-century war efforts concentrated on hard-science and management skills, global COIN must summon and use many disciplines, including psychology, forensics political science, linguistics, and anthropology. The key, again, is to recognize that the threat cannot be countered without more brainpower.

Following the devastating attacks of 9/11, the United States instinctively, and understandably, concentrated on firepower to prevent repeat attacks and to destroy those who could conduct them. But instinct is not strategy. Reliance on firepower has not enabled the United States to reverse the globalizing Salafist tide. Every use of force against Muslims, not to mention every misuse, is employed by the adversary to make the case to militants and prospective martyrs that their community needs them to fight and die. While firepower has a place in global COIN, it cannot substitute for improved abilities to take away the advantage the Salafists currently hold on the cognitive plane. To defeat an enemy that has figured out how to use U.S. military power to perpetuate itself, it will take the best thinking that can be marshaled.

---

[10] Bird and Sherwin (2005).

CHAPTER FOUR
Thoughts of the Jihad

We are now ready to examine challenges of global insurgency on the cognitive level. The first task in this examination is to understand the adversary's core strength. In John Mackinlay's words, "The logic of counter strategy would be to know more about and focus on the opponents' source of energy . . . rather than his proxy battlefields."[1] For the global Salafist insurgency, this "source of energy" is the ability to create, sustain, and channel intense *individual* motivation. The jihad relies on spirituality and reasoning more than on structural order, physical and electronic capabilities, or territorial control. Physical means of terror are technically simple, readily available, and largely incidental. Hijacked airliners did not bring down the World Trade Center towers any more than the combination of personalized holy war and intelligent planning did. The reasoning that leads to the decision to attack, the resourcefulness of plans of attack, and the final willpower to attack are harder to counter than the weapons used.

More than traditional national insurgencies, worldwide jihad has otherworldly motivations. Much—too much—has been made of the enticement of bountiful rewards awaiting each martyr in paradise. A more important Salafist theme is that recovery of the piety of early ancestral Muslims is a cause worth fighting for. This positive, if vague, incentive is coupled with a more immediate and negative one: the belief that Islam, in its true form, has been targeted for annihilation by Christians and Jews—a cause worth killing and dying for.

Holy war is a specific idea. It does not figure in every conflict involving confessional identity.[2] Holy war is not the same as sectarian wars in which contending political agendas coincide with religious divisions or persecution, as in Northern Ireland, the Balkan wars, and much of South Asia's Hindu-Muslim violence. Muslim-Christian tensions in sub-Saharan Africa do not signify that jihad is sweeping across the region (though the possibility cannot be excluded). Even in Iraq, where jihadis are active, Sunni-Shiite antagonism has more to do with who rules the country than with which is the legitimate branch of Islam.

In contrast, the prime mover of jihad is religion:

The theological concept that every Muslim is part of the Ummah (One Muslim Nation) that was used as far back as the 10th Century in an attempt to bring some unity to support the Sunni creed has gained great currency in contemporary political Islamist movements.

---

[1] Mackinlay and Al-Baddawy (forthcoming).

[2] Examples of genuine holy war include the conflicts associated with early Islamic expansion, the Crusades, and the Hundred Years' War, all of which had mainly, though not solely, theological motivations.

It means that if any Muslim comes under attack, it is the religious duty of others to defend him in whatever way is appropriate.[3]

With this as the precept, it remains for jihadist propagandists to convince potential fighters that Muslims are in fact under attack.

To that end, the jihadists produce "evidence" of Western-Christian-Jewish aggression against Islam and the ummah: U.S. military presence in the land of the Prophet since 1991, invasion and subsequent military operations against Sunnis in Iraq, extrajudicial detention of Muslims in secret prisons, support for Israeli oppression of Palestinians, support for apostate regimes, anti-Muslim discrimination in the West. With such grist, al Qaeda's propaganda mill runs with great productivity. For instance, one Muslim described Guantanamo as a "place where Muslims are routinely tortured." The case need not convince everyone because jihad only needs intense commitment from relatively few Muslims. The strong sense of individual jihadist duty to protect the ummah by striking back against those who harm it should register a warning against any approach to COIN that relies heavily on the use of force against Muslims.

Where Salafism takes on more practical political agendas (in Iraq, Palestine, Pakistan, Chechnya, Egypt, and Southeast Asia, for example), it is because it can align itself with local rebel or separatist causes with at least temporarily compatible goals. To jihad strategists, national causes are stepping stones toward a more grandiose vision—and chances to cause greater mayhem. The involvement of jihadis from many countries in local insurgencies shows that they regard each one as part of a larger war. Gaining governmental power in any nation-state is neither sufficient nor necessary for the conduct of that war. "[T]he Jewish-Crusader alliance, led by the United States, will not allow any Muslim force to reach power in any of the Islamic countries."[4]

As noted, one of the most important and perplexing aspects of the global insurgency is that it does not rely on or seek territorial control as national insurgencies do. True, some Muslim lands, e.g., Saudi Arabia, are considered holier than others, and some, e.g., Iraq, have special strategic importance. However, the underlying jihadist rationale—that the global Muslim community is under attack and its defenders must strike back wherever they can— makes territorial and governmental control relatively unimportant.

Because the Muslim community is not conterminous with political boundaries, violent Salafism treats territorial specificity, like physical capabilities, as incidental. As Secretary of Defense Rumsfeld has observed, the fact that jihad has no territory to defend makes it harder, not easier, to combat.[5] For the individual jihadi, the decoupling of religion from state and the estrangement of the individual from the state have led to a "de-territorialized version of Islam."[6] Geographically unfettered, jihad can recruit individuals to join, travel, migrate, burrow, wait,

---

[3] Mackinlay and Al-Baddawy (forthcoming); emphasis in original.

[4] Ayman al-Zawahiri, quoted in Pape (2005).

[5] Rumsfeld (2006). His observation is more convincing than National Intelligence Director John Negroponte's view that the lack of territorial control by al Qaeda in Iraq is an indicator of U.S. military success. (See Negroponte, 2006.)

[6] Olivier Roy, cited in Mackinlay (2005).

scheme, and attack virtually anywhere. While jihadis welcome geographic sanctuary, as they enjoy in western Pakistan, it is as a base from which to operate rather than a political end in itself. They may even hope that the Sunni heartland of Iraq will become such a safe haven, but they learned the perils of reliance on territory when the United States swept through Afghanistan. Moreover, the small groups operating under the banner of jihad in urban Western Europe and North America need no sanctuary beyond their apartments, their anonymity, and their computers.

The United States government is now fixated on al Qaeda's stated goal of creating a new caliphate: a geopolitical (oil-rich) entity in which Muslims can live the pious life free from injustice, harm, and trespassing infidels. As the U.S. rationale for the war in Iraq has migrated from eliminating an interstate threat to combating jihad, U.S. policymakers have warned that the alternative to victory there could be the birth of this caliphate. They may take this more seriously than do the jihadis themselves, for whom the caliphatic vision appears to be utopian, not practical. In fact, it is less useful for motivating militants and martyrs than the claim that Muslims are threatened in *today's* world. In the words of a leading scholar of Islam and jihad, Olivier Roy, "The concept of a world Muslim ummah as a geopolitical actor is nonsense."[7]

The indifference of jihadis to political rule, in the conventional sense, is apparent in how they perform when actually in control of a state or city. Given a chance to govern, the best that the Taliban and their "Arab guests" could do in Afghanistan was to bully anyone who strayed from strict Islamic law. They were evidently more concerned with cleansing the population of impurity than with creating a functional state. In Fallujah, following the failed first attempt by U.S. Marines to take the city by force in April 2004, "governance" consisted mainly of roaming jihadis, foreign and Iraqi, intimidating shopkeepers and women without regard to such matters as disposing of trash, much less building a viable stronghold. In general, jihadis lack the experience, interest, and skills to exercise sovereignty as we define it.

As far as we know, jihadis have no plans or conception of how to organize, govern, and defend a country, much less a vast Islamic realm.[8] "Beyond the simplistic notion of imposing a caliphate, . . . the leaders of the organization appear never to have thought about the most basic facts of government. What kind of economic model would they follow? How would they cope with unemployment? . . . The truth . . . is that radical Islamists have no interest in government; they are interested only in jihad."[9]

Making the assumption that the immediate objective of the global Salafist insurgency is to seize government and then exercise territorial sovereignty can lead to inappropriate COIN strategies, tactics, and capabilities, e.g., large-scale occupations, assaults to regain control of cities, and menacing armored columns. By the same token, we should take no comfort in the jihad's limited chances of actually seizing one or more nation-states. It does not need to do so to threaten U.S. and allied interests, safety, and way of life and the international order. Jihad's deterritorialization compounds its complexity—its limitless cells, locations, contingen-

---

[7] Roy (2006, pp. 268–269).

[8] In this respect, they are different from other aggressive ideologies, such as early communism and national socialism, which had clear notions of how society should function.

[9] Wright (2006).

cies, tributaries, and targets—and thus the analytical, strategic, and operational challenges of global COIN.

This is not the first time the United States has faced a global adversary that aids and uses local movements. It was the stock scenario of communist expansionism during the Cold War, from Central America to Indochina. Fidel Castro's legions conducted or supported insurgencies in a number of Latin American and African countries. On the whole, this Soviet strategy produced meager results, either because of Soviet clumsiness, because local insurgents failed, or because they could not be manipulated by Moscow. As was learned belatedly, the Vietnamese were moved by national liberation and unity far more than by international Marxism. The Viet Cong and North Vietnamese were more complex than was understood by U.S. intelligence, and U.S. one-size-fits-all tactics did not work. Yet, compared to al Qaeda, the enemy in Vietnam was simple—linear in behavior, confined in location, and straightforward in objectives.

To the extent that it can tap into religious fundamentalism, anger, and fear, global jihad can gain more influence with local Islamic causes than Moscow could with local communists. Al Qaeda's ability to fashion and project a common ideology is superior to that of the Kremlin's dull denizens. At the same time, the U.S. tendency to homogenize the Salafist threat in rhetoric and strategy can be counterproductive (as it often was vis-à-vis communist movements during the Cold War).[10] Treating all political Islamists, Muslim insurgents, and religious radicals as holy warriors plays directly into al Qaeda's hands by strengthening links among movements and expanding the recruiting pool. Violence against nonviolent Islamists—sending forces into mosques, for example—fits the story that Islam is under assault.

Jihad has multiple tiers, from personal jihad to separatist insurgencies to Islamist opposition to conservative Arab regimes to militancy among disaffected Muslims in Europe to global terrorism. COIN must be waged on as many tiers, from promoting reform of Arab states to isolating Islamist militants amidst larger Muslim populations to countering terrorism perpetrated by jihadist cells in the West. The jihad's complex agenda—to protect Muslims and Islam, to establish a new caliphate, to evict U.S. forces from Muslim holy lands, to kill infidels—complicates goal-setting for COIN. Such complexity underscores the imperative of major and sustained investment in analytical capabilities as part of a greater emphasis on the cognitive domain.

Jihad is at once universal and personal.[11] The combination of devotion to the worldwide Muslim community and individual rage that the community is under siege, often mixed with humiliating personal experience, can lead to extreme acts.[12] The need for such intense motivation places a premium on the charisma of leaders, whether in the haunting visage of bin Laden, the arresting words of al-Zawahiri, or the sheer brutality of the late Abu Musab al-Zarqawi. They know that the expanse of their appeal to radicalism is less important than the intensity of their appeal to violence for the individual already radicalized. It took the better part of a year (2003–2004) before the U.S. command in Iraq understood that the number of foreign terror-

[10] Kilcullen (2005).

[11] The intensely personal nature of holy war is captured in the analysis of global insurgency by John Mackinlay of King's College, London. (See Mackinlay, 2005.)

[12] International Crisis Group (2006a).

ists operating in Iraq was relatively unimportant: Their capability and leverage lay in the intensity of their personal commitment, as well as their organizational skills, their willingness to commit unrestrained violence, and their ability to recruit suicide bombers (including Iraqis).

COIN efforts to turn moderate Muslim populations against terrorism, while not unimportant, do not get at the heart of the problem of stopping the intensely motivated jihadi who makes a personal decision to commit acts that others consider heinous but he—or, lately, she—considers heroic.[13] Any model that overlooks jihadis' morality, as they see it, will fail. In their story, the U.S. and its allies are the ones who have forsaken morality. This resonates with a majority of Muslims who see Westerners as "selfish" and "immoral."[14] The harmony of violence and ethics in the mindset of jihadis and their supporters is evident in the community-mindedness and incorruptibility of some violent Islamist groups, e.g., Hamas and Hezbollah.

For U.S. policymakers to brand jihad as "anti-freedom" may be useful for winning backing for policies *at home*. And it certainly is true that liberty and individual rights, as U.S. convention defines them, have no place in Salafism. At the same time, it is important to understand that many Muslims, not just violent ones, place a higher value on justice than on freedom. Injustice toward Muslims is viewed as a form of assault that warrants a jihadist response. Whether in the life of the Prophet, sacred texts, or contemporary Islamic commentary, there is little to suggest a yearning for representative government, yet there is much to suggest a feeling of inequity in treatment and in wealth. COIN analysis, strategy, and action must take seriously the broad appeal of al Qaeda's claim that the West's affinity for democracy is hypocritical and a pretext for treating Muslims as inferior. If the West's preferred weapon in the war of ideas is to convince Muslims of the virtues of democracy, it will have to explain why democracy has left millions of Muslims on the margin of European society.

The demand for justice is the backdrop against which Muslims view footage of humiliated prisoners and wailing mothers. Dismissing the ethical construct of jihad, as opposed to condemning its violence, is unlikely to advance global COIN. The idea of heroic defenders of an embattled community is a powerful one not only for jihadis. The belief that all but a small fraction of Muslims see things as the West does is wishful. Glorification of martyrdom operations against the home of the Crusaders is not confined to the martyrs themselves. "[F]or many Muslims, the thrall of the Ummah is stronger than [the] vision of civil society."[15]

Because of the widespread feeling of injustice against Muslims, it will not be easy to isolate the jihadis, much less cause the peaceable majority to turn against them. Muslim tolerance of Islamist violence is a major problem. "The moderate Muslim majority . . . only has to do nothing for the insurgency to survive in its midst."[16] The jihadis do not depend on the active support of nonextremists, only that they do not report them to Western security and intelligence services. A major cognitive challenge is thus to find the right voice to activate the contested population against violent jihad in Muslim-majority as well as Muslim-minority

---

[13] Devji (2005).

[14] Pew Global Attitudes Project (2006).

[15] Mackinlay and Al-Baddawy (forthcoming).

[16] Mackinlay and Al-Baddawy (forthcoming).

countries. "Adopting a counter-strategy assumes a degree of knowledge we do not have about the communications paths by which extremist ideology reaches its target, about the size of the European minorities and more important what percentage of them are vaguely of strongly sympathetic to jihadist views."[17]

The combination of widespread Muslim disaffection and the potency of the call to duty of a fanatical few means that jihadist terrorism can occur virtually anywhere. "The ruling to kill Americans . . . civilians and military . . . is an individual duty for every Muslim who can do it in any country in which it is possible to do it."[18] Nationalism, separatism, and even tribalism have discernible boundaries, and this aids in understanding and countering insurgencies rooted in such -isms. There was no reason to fear Vietnamese attacks in the United States or elsewhere far from Vietnam. In contrast, angry Muslims in Europe and the United States are no less attractive candidates for jihad than are those in the Arab heartland—harder to recruit, perhaps, but more dangerous once recruited. This compounds the problem of distinguishing jihadis from harmless and blameless Muslims (and even from non-Muslims, as we know from the tragic case of the terrified young Brazilian immigrant who was gunned down by police in the London Underground). Iraq and Afghanistan teach us that finding jihadis is harder than eliminating them once found, and finding them is as much a cognitive challenge as a technical challenge.[19]

Global COIN should treat intense spiritual motivation as a real jihadist *capability*: a resonant cognitive frequency that can cause people to take extraordinarily destructive and self-destructive acts, yielding immense operational advantages for the jihad.[20] The possibility of suicide attacks, difficult to prevent in the best of circumstances, nearly anywhere and any time renders inadequate COIN based on physical weapons, hierarchical organization, and territorial control. Methods to prevent suicide attacks rely heavily on effective cognition and shortening the time from warning to decision to action. But improved prevention of specific acts will not alone reduce the danger. The ability of Salafi propagandists, often abetted by sympathetic clerics, to sustain suicide war through relentless recruitment makes global COIN challenging and frustrating. If we do not understand why and how such recruitment works, perpetuation of jihad cannot be stopped. Indeed, its perpetuation may even be abetted.

It may be useful to consider a jihadist "personnel model" (as depicted in Figure 4.1) that connects the injustice, oppression, or harm felt by a great many Muslims with the martyrdom chosen by a few. Like any model, this one is not meant to reproduce reality but only to represent it faithfully yet simply. Jihadist propagandists understand the propensity for grievance among Muslims everywhere, the possibility that the aggrieved can be radicalized by clerics and peers, the short distance between radicalization and militancy, the conversion of militant radicals into jihadis, and the final step of turning a jihadi into a martyr.

---

[17] Mackinlay and Al-Baddawy (forthcoming).

[18] 1998 al Qaeda fatwa issued by bin Laden and al-Zawahiri.

[19] This is an important finding of the newly completed U.S. DoD Quadrennial Defense Review.

[20] Suicide bombing is an especially destructive and dangerous weapon because it can be targeted with precision, does not require escape, and spreads a sense of horror, as Bruce Hoffman has articulated. (See Hoffman, 2005.)

Figure 4.1
The Jihadist Personnel Model

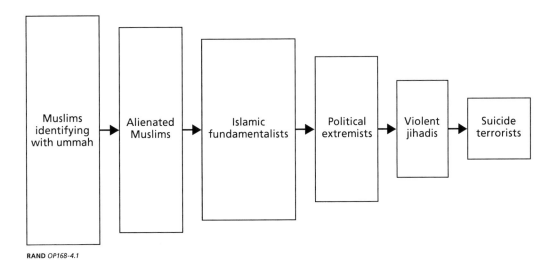

RAND *OP168-4.1*

The psychology of this process boils down to a search for virtue.[21] Even as Western populations speak of the evil of jihad, its fighters see themselves as graduating toward greater goodness and purity as they make the journey from anger to martyrdom—a belief that intensifies over the course of the journey. The force that moves individuals along that path is cognitive. Although there are indications that some individuals are induced to become jihadis and martyrs by promises of payments to their families or by pressure, most are uncoerced.

The process in the model begins with the widely held sense of one community transcending nation-states. To that is added a feeling, fanned by propaganda, that the community is threatened, which gives rise to anger and frustration. The antidote offered for such anger and frustration is religious fundamentalism. "Alienation from citizenship . . . and a loss of faith in secular opportunity create a pool of potential volunteers; preachers, recruiters, and Al Qaeda leaders take it from there."[22] Of those attracted to fundamentalism, some will accept a personal duty to act, making them candidates for militancy, extremism, and violence. The few who are called to ultimate sacrifice are prepared to commit horrific and self-destructive acts. Only a fraction of individuals pass from one stage to the next, starting with a billion Muslims and culminating with perhaps a few thousand individuals in the queue for martyrdom. But again, suicide terrorism is such that only a few are needed.

The case of Mohammad Sidique Khan, ringleader of the suicide bomber attacks in London on July 7, 2005, is indicative of this model. A well-liked teacher's aide and British citizen, Kahn lost his job, renounced his British identity, enlisted in a jihadist militia, and promptly began planning the London bombings. His posthumous video statement established the culpability of those who had been his fellow citizens and became his victims: "Your democratically elected

---

[21] In this respect, jihad as holy war is similar to jihad as a quest for personal betterment.

[22] Coll (2006).

government continuously perpetuate[s] atrocities against *my people all over the world*" (emphasis added). For Kahn, the distance from disaffection to suicide terror was quickly traversed.[23]

There is no more crucial or difficult challenge in global COIN than interrupting the progression from frustration to faith to terror, as represented in the model in Figure 4.1. The use of force against any segment along the way can reinforce the process by validating the argument that the ummah and Islamic purity are being attacked by a physically stronger power and therefore require heroic jihadis to defend them. Interfering with the progression from Muslim to martyr is thus better done with brainpower than firepower, as will be discussed later.

Notwithstanding its religious, ethical, and emotional aspects, jihad also relies heavily on the disciplined reasoning of its intellectuals and operatives, who include persons with considerable creative, analytical, and intuitive powers. Some are good at planning sophisticated operations; some at outsmarting, adapting to, and navigating through COIN measures; some at motivational tactics in support of the holy war. Al-Zawahiri is a prime example of the mix of intellectual agility, strategic focus, and religious fire. The combination of cognitive skills and spiritual resonance is especially potent when distributed amongst individuals and small cells connected by networks around the world.

It is in vogue to think of al Qaeda not as an organization but as some sort of virus, lacking a skeletal structure and central nervous system. If so, its cognitive capability would be reactive and opportunistic but not strategic. Another interpretation is offered by RAND researcher David Ronfeldt: "The deeper reality may be that it is . . . *deliberately* shifting its shape and style to suit changing circumstances, including the addition of new, semi-autonomous affiliates to the broader network."[24] This suggests not only intent but also a continuing cognitive center, though not necessarily one that is fixed and concentrated organizationally or geographically: It is a distributed jihad with a distributed mind.

The global Salafist insurgency does have an intelligent network structure with operational advantages. Charismatic figures at the core supply a message bearing rage, shared ideology, and a call to jihad. Operating hubs provide financial, planning, communications, logistical, and other support and direction to fighters along the spokes. While the insurgency has assumed this form at least in part because U.S.-led attacks since 9/11 have forced it to do so, the effect is to make it harder to defeat through traditional COIN.

Among its advantages, this structure serves the jihadist strategy of gaining local affiliates. Just as Iraq's Sunni insurgency has become increasingly Islamist since 2004, so may the Palestinian cause join with radical Islam. Hamas draws on religious zeal to advance a political agenda and to recruit and motivate martyrs, and it surely has been targeted by al Qaeda as a promising local ally.[25] To the extent that jihadist ideology gains ground among Palestinians, a "two-state" solution could lose its appeal with them because the existence of a Zionist state is incompatible with jihad's central purposes. In general, jihad offers a thematic coupling between the ferocity of peoples defending their homelands and the fervor of believers defend-

---

[23] Coll (2006).

[24] Ronfeldt (2005); emphasis added.

[25] The Hamas charter of 1988 states, "If an enemy invades Muslim territories, then Jihad and fighting the enemy becomes the individual duty of every Muslim" (Hamas, 1988).

ing their religion—two powerful human impulses.[26] The skill to create shared consciousness is as important as any capability possessed by the brain trust of the jihad.

Hezbollah is another example of an Islamist insurgency that is both local and transnational. As Henry Kissinger has written,

> We are witnessing a carefully conceived assault . . . on the international system of respect for sovereignty and territorial integrity. The creation of organizations like Hezbollah and al Qaeda symbolizes that transnational loyalties are replacing national ones. The driving force behind this challenge is the jihadist conviction that it is the existing order that is illegitimate. . . . For the jihad's adherents, the battlefield cannot be defined by frontiers based on principles of world order they reject; what we call terror is, to the jihadists, an act of war to undermine illegitimate regimes.[27]

That Hezbollah is a Shia-based, Iran-backed radical movement, not a Sunni-Salafist one, further complicates the problem of understanding these phenomena. Are we witnessing a civil war or an alliance between Sunnis and Shias?

Both the spiritual and cognitive components of jihadist capabilities depend on the availability and use of networked information. Without global connectivity and media, it would be difficult to conspire and cooperate while distributed. Jihadis comprise sophisticated users and engineers of information, and they stress information engineering and user skills in personnel recruitment and development.[28] They are creatures of the Internet and exploiters of the media. They are as good at anonymity as they are at attracting the spotlight, and they take information security very seriously.[29]

Jihadis use networked information not only to conspire and cooperate but also, as Bruce Hoffman explains, to resonate [with], recruit, and regenerate candidates for suicide strikes. It is the capacity for repetitive suicide bombings that casts a constant shadow on our security and ways of life. Effective global COIN must therefore address the jihadist life cycle (more accurately, death cycle), not only dissuading resentful Muslims from becoming militant but also stopping militants from becoming terrorists.

Jihad leaders might not be as concerned as we think with winning broad popular support in the Muslim world.[30] They appeal to those who, already alienated, will not be offended, and may even be impressed, by violence. Al Qaeda uses acts of martyrdom to generate new martyrs and footage of beheadings to inspire more beheadings. Just as attacks *on* Muslims are treated as the reason to wage holy war, attacks *by* Muslims are seen as proof that holy war against U.S. power is not futile. Meanwhile, perceived injustice and violence toward Muslims, includ-

---

[26] This is consistent with the research of Robert Pape, which links suicide terrorism with perceptions of foreign aggression and occupation.

[27] Kissinger (2006).

[28] Gunaratna (2002).

[29] It remains to be seen whether they will adopt information warfare as a complement to terrorism. While they could develop the capability to do this, it might not fit their holy-war mindset.

[30] On this there may be a difference of opinion between those like al-Zawahiri who place some value on broad support and those like al-Zarqawi who consider Shi'a and apostate or secular Sunnis fair game.

ing as part of COIN, replenishes the stock of disaffected fundamentalists from which jihadis are drawn. That the U.S. military in Iraq detained an estimated two noninsurgents for every three real insurgents rounded up in the first year of occupation expanded and radicalized the insurgency. It seems that jihadists leave it to the West to alienate Muslims in large numbers, enabling them to concentrate on turning alienation into the will to kill and die.

The key intellectual challenge in global COIN is to figure out how to weaken the jihadis' ability, through motivation and manipulation, to follow each suicide attack with another. Given the size of the pool, U.S. "public diplomacy" and "strategic communications" to win over the larger Muslim population may be of marginal value in stemming the perpetuation of jihad, which depends mainly on the choices of a relatively few, already militant persons. When more than a third of American Muslims—known for their moderation—believe that their own government is "fighting a war on Islam," one can begin to fathom the difficulty of persuading non-American Muslims that this is not the case.[31]

Dissuading extremists from becoming terrorists, and thus degrading the ability of jihad to resonate, recruit and regenerate, cannot be achieved by criticizing the religious beliefs of millions upon millions of Muslim fundamentalists, violent or not, any more than by relying mainly on the use of force. Rather, it will take a sophisticated strategy that depends on making sense of and using abundant information in understanding, shaping, and operating. This does not mean imitating the religious rage and manipulative techniques of the jihad. It means knowing jihad and depriving it of its advantages on that level.

The cognitive challenge of global COIN should not be underestimated. Against an adversary that fans and exploits Muslims' beliefs that both their community and faith are under attack, neither a war of bullets nor a war of ideas can be waged without the risk of making things worse. Yet both bullets and ideas are needed in global COIN. The challenge is to know when, where, with whom, by whom, and how to use them. This is why it is not enough to say that COIN has to become smarter without embarking on a strategy to make it so.

---

[31] Zogby International (2004, p. 27).

CHAPTER FIVE

Closing the Gap

The cognitive challenge of global insurgency raises questions about the adequacy and applicability of the "standard model" of COIN, with its stress on structures (organizations, forces), physical-electronic capabilities (weapons, sensors, facilities), and control of real estate. For starters, we need to understand that an attritional strategy will not work. The enemy wants, even needs the United States and its allies to pursue an attritional strategy because attacks on any part of the ummah help sustain the jihad and justify suicidal counterattacks.

Three years of operations by the U.S. military to secure the Sunni Triangle have had little effect on the ability of foreign and Iraqi jihadis to conduct bold terrorist operations against Iraqi Shias and Iraqi security forces, bringing the country to, if not over, the brink of civil war. As of this writing, it does not seem that al-Zarqawi's death has reduced this threat. Even without al-Zarqawi, segments of the indigenous Sunni insurgency have taken on jihadist motivations and methods, making them harder to defeat with traditional military structures, weapons, territorial control, and attrition for the reasons already presented here.

The deficiency of traditional COIN is even more obvious in the face of a global insurgency that does not rely on national insurgencies. Global jihad is active not only in tandem with local insurgencies but also where there are no local insurgencies remotely capable of overthrowing national government—the United Kingdom, France, the Netherlands, Spain, Canada, the United States—the aim being not to seize government but to change government policy and to earn support in the ummah by striking back at its attackers. In such cases, military force, territorial control, and other methods of classical COIN are largely irrelevant.

As Figure 5.1 illustrates, if the preoccupation with structural and physical COIN capabilities and territorial control (see right side of figure) has not been entirely suitable for countering traditional insurgency (on the left side of the figure), what chance does it have against globalized insurgency (in the center of the figure)?[1] Not much.

We have noted the connection between the cognitive and the spiritual within global jihad. In COIN, the *distinction* between cognition and religion is critical. COIN must not try to battle jihadist motivations with religious argumentation, since this can validate the Salafists' story and increase the perception, and possibly the reality, of a Christian-Muslim holy war—precisely what jihadis want. Use of any term that evokes the image of Crusade is especially harmful not only in offending Muslims but also in suggesting that the purpose of COIN

---

[1]   A companion analysis will examine the information-capabilities layer of 21st-century COIN.

Figure 5.1
COIN Capabilities Profile

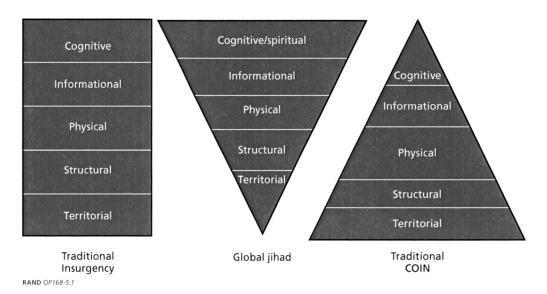

operations is religious combat. The stakes are very high. Many Muslims feel that they are part of a religious community that has been targeted. Islamic fundamentalism is on the rise not only, and not primarily, because of the call to jihad. All that has to be done to swell the pool of militants and potential martyrs is to echo the story of holy war that inspires jihad. COIN should avoid any hint of religious motivation.

Does this mean that global COIN on the cognitive level should exclude a "war of ideas"? Yes and no. It is important to distinguish violent extremist insurgency from the much larger number of Muslims who have a distaste for Western culture and hold fundamentalist beliefs. This population cannot easily be convinced to accept liberal designs for society. It is equally counterproductive for the United States to suggest its preferred brand of Islam, compatible with modernity, democracy, and U.S. interests.[2] Thus, in a war of ideas, it is not clear what ideas in the U.S. arsenal can be effective and are free of risk.

A critical question for cognitive COIN is *where* in the jihadist personnel model (described earlier) the progression from Muslim belief to martyrdom can be interrupted. Where the jihadist argument is weakest has to do not with political philosophy, social injustice, or cultural contamination but with killing. In particular, the claims of violent Salafists that the Koran sanctions the killing of one's self, innocents, and other Muslims are flimsy.[3] Reputable Islamic scholars insist on a Koranic prohibition of all three of these categories of killing.[4] Yet, again, for

---

[2] Scheuer (2004).

[3] Hafez (2006).

[4] Consider, for example the Fiqh of North America Fatwa of July 27, 2005: "Islam strictly condemns . . . the use of violence against innocent lives. There is no justification in Islam for . . . terrorism. Targeting civilians' life and property through suicide bombings or any other method of attack . . . is forbidden—and those who commit these barbaric acts are criminals, not 'martyrs'" (Council on American-Islamic Relations, 2005).

the U.S. government and non-Muslims to suggest religious interpretations to convince radicalized Muslims not to become terrorists is perilous and ineffectual. They can try to encourage some Muslims (e.g., non-jihadist yet fundamentalist clerics) to present an alternative religious interpretation, though any direct and explicit support could anger other Muslims, validate the Salafists, and discredit non-jihadis.[5] Similarly, it may be fruitless for Americans or any non-Muslims to demonize acts that jihadis and their supporters consider righteous.[6] Only Muslim condemnation will work, and then only partly, given that terrorists are typically radicals already. On the whole, COIN is more likely to succeed to the extent it (1) contradicts the Salafists' narrative of ummah under attack; (2) concentrates the use of force on jihadist killers; and (3) respects all forms of Islam, including fundamentalism, provided they are nonviolent.

Recent public opinion polls bear out the idea that it is easier to separate violent Islamists from nonviolent ones than it is to prevent Muslims from embracing radical political and religious attitudes. A majority of Muslims feel aggrieved and embittered toward the West, and these attitudes have grown worse in recent years. During the same time, there has been a substantial decline in Muslim support for terrorism against civilians to defend Islam, with a sizeable majority saying that it can never be justified.[7]

There is an undeniable need to maintain *domestic* support for global COIN: cohesion, perseverance, and resolve to defend democratic values and ways of life. However, domestic words, before uttered, must be weighed for their potential effects on the perpetuation of jihad. Demonizing Islamic fundamentalism, however tempting and gratifying, is not needed to gain domestic support for COIN, which should be based on concern for security, not on hatred. It risks being interpreted as a condemnation of Islam.

If emotions and rhetoric concerning jihad affect rationality in analyzing, crafting strategy, and making decisions, a price will be payed. As one senior British officer has written of his experience in Iraq, "High levels of emotivity . . . serve to distort collective judgment and invoke responses to insurgent activity that ultimately exacerbated the situation."[8] A lack of objectivity in analysis and decisions risks helping the jihad gain more support and recruits than it would otherwise. Moreover, Salafist extremism is predicated in part on a claim that U.S. attacks on Islam are religiously inspired. For these reasons, we should omit the spiritual layer from the capabilities for global COIN, even though it is a jihadist capability.

Generally speaking, the jihad is better at making sense and use of available information relative to *its* strategy than current COIN is relative to *its* strategy. Lacking comparable technology and firepower, the jihadist leadership places a higher priority on cognitive effectiveness and is ready to pounce on mistakes. The most common and costly mental mistake in COIN is the brandishing of U.S. military power. In bin Laden's words, "Americans have com-

---

[5] Egyptian authorities have done this well.

[6] Winston Churchill is often cited as the model wartime leader. However, his incessant message of the sheer evil of Hitler was intended to make the British people resolute, not to cause the German people to rise up against their leadership. While it is unclear what effects his domestic rhetoric had on German attitudes, it is best to assume that for non-Muslim figures to accuse Muslims of any ilk of being evil will hurt more than help COIN.

[7] Pew Global Attitudes Project (2006).

[8] Alwyn-Foster (2005, p. 6).

mitted unprecedented stupidity. They have attacked Islam and its most significant sacrosanct symbols."[9] Although jihadis have much less information available to them than U.S. agencies and services involved in COIN do, they make better use of the information they have. The jihad is more adept at networking, in the nontechnical sense, than are U.S. security services. It is flatter, more flexible, more open to learning, and vastly more economical.

This gap is exacerbated by the fact that the national security establishment of the U.S. government has been a straggler in the strategic use of information since the early days of networked computing. Along with improving cognitive capabilities there must be progress in gathering, fusing, moving, and providing unobstructed access to information for COIN. Habits of controlling networks and compartmentalizing data in U.S. national security organizations—the need-to-know culture—hinder access to information for those who need it and obstruct horizontal collaboration during operations. Though not careless, al Qaeda has no such institutionalized barriers to the flow of information.

Evidence of jihad's advantage in using information can be found at the strategic, operational, and tactical levels. Strategically, jihad has shocked and affected Western democracies beyond its actual capability to do damage. It has provoked attack, which it uses as further proof of the need for jihad and martyrdom. It can open up more "fronts" than may be effectively handled: numerous potential homeland security threats, support for insurgency in Iraq, subversion of conservative Arab regimes, and unpredictable terrorism from Bali to Basra to Britain. This requires COIN to answer jihad's millions of dollars in costs with hundreds of billions of its own. The asymmetric economies of global insurgency and COIN are the product of al Qaeda's resourcefulness and U.S. preference for complex organizations and heavy equipment. Moreover, out of regard for jihadist ingenuity and lack of inhibition, the United States must spend heavily for protection against capabilities jihadis *might* acquire, such as weapons of mass destruction.

Operationally, jihad adapts well to countermeasures. For instance, having largely shut down the use of airliners as weapons (by blocking cockpit access), there is now a growing frequency of pedestrian and vehicle suicide bomb attacks. Tactically, its cells and individuals can move and act in hours when COIN can take days to react.[10] Such advantages are less the result of detailed guidance from some cave-headquarters than of the nature of the insurgency: its ability to resonate ideologically with, recruit, and regenerate violent radicals; its geographic diffusiveness; its mobility; its decentralization of initiative and authority; and its tolerance of randomness in the acts of its adherents.[11] The sluggishness of U.S. COIN operations is mainly the product of top-down decisionmaking and institutional impediments to sharing information and collaboration across organizational boundaries.

---

[9] Miller (1998).

[10] The speed with which fresh information led to the fateful air strike on al-Zarqawi's headquarters in June 2006, suggests, at least anecdotally, that this is improving.

[11] Devji (2005).

In sum, global jihad taxes the cognitive capabilities of COIN in several respects:

- Its capability to manipulate and seize control of the minds of militants and turn their bodies into weapons is difficult to counter with organizational and physical means.[12]
- Its complexity and instability make analysis, strategy, and operational decisionmaking more difficult than for familiar nation-state COIN.
- The jihad's lack of territorial definition and the difficulty of distinguishing jihadis from other military-age Muslims make locating threats a daunting problem.
- This is an intellectually formidable enemy that excels in using information.
- It learns from both its mistakes and those of COIN.
- Unencumbered by bureaucracy, tradition, government procurement regulations, and other burdens and rigidities, it adapts to its environment and reacts to COIN at speeds that frustrate COIN.

The United States can do much better on the cognitive level of COIN. It needs to make more productive use of the information its own technology and infrastructure provide and to invest purposefully and programmatically in becoming more sophisticated in analysis, wiser in strategy, and smarter in operational decisionmaking.

---

[12] It is interesting to consider what course World War II in the Pacific would have taken if Japan had had an inexhaustible supply of kamikaze pilots and planes. Unless the ability of jihad to resonate with, recruit, and regenerate suicide bombers can be broken, the supply may well be inexhaustible.

CHAPTER SIX

Cognitive Requirements in Global COIN

Thus far, this paper has made the case for reordering priorities among the capabilities the United States uses to counter the global Salafist insurgency, placing more stress on cognitive and less on technological and physical capabilities, organizational structure, territorial control, and attritional strategy. It has explained that, with popular sympathy in the balance, knowing when, where, how, by whom, and against whom to apply deadly force in COIN is extremely important and demanding. Finally, to set the stage for defining needed cognitive capabilities, this paper has described the jihadist challenge on this level: complex, distributed, connected, elusive, dynamic, and skilled in recruiting fighters and martyrs based on a story of Islam under attack.

Before detailing the cognitive capabilities needed to meet this challenge, a short excursion into basic requirements for COIN decisionmaking is necessary. In brief, those engaged in decisionmaking under critical conditions should be capable of

- *reliable intuition*, based on experience and established mental models
- *sound reasoning*, based on a logical weighing of fresh information and interesting options, unconstrained by established models
- *strong self-awareness*, in order to understand how to balance and combine intuition and reasoning.[1]

Why this particular cognitive "package"? Research shows that decisionmakers rely overwhelmingly on intuition, as opposed to reasoning, when conditions are dangerous or otherwise critical and time is short. This holds true for firefighters, hospital personnel, and those in other high-pressure professions, including soldiers and others involved in security operations. Yet conditions prevalent in 21st-century COIN raise questions about such heavy reliance on intuition in time-sensitive decisionmaking:

- Intuition is based heavily on experience, yet COIN often presents unfamiliar circumstances.
- Because COIN is so complex—moreso than regular warfare because of the ambiguity of force—that intuition based on simplified mental models of reality may not suffice.

---

[1] Gompert, Lachow, and Perkins (2005).

- By making fresh information readily available, information networking can reduce dependence on experience-based intuition.

In essence, it is no longer wise or necessary to rely almost exclusively on intuition to make urgent COIN decisions. Unstable conditions demand and networked information permits expanded reliance on reasoning, even when time is short. Effective cognition in critical decisionmaking demands the *integration* of intuition and reasoning, which in turn demands high self-awareness. To reinforce a point made earlier, improved cognition is not about sensors, chat rooms, search engines, and visual displays, but about intuition, reasoning, and self-awareness inside the cortex once humans receive information.

What makes effective cognition so difficult in countering global insurgency is the diminishing utility of the mental models on which COIN relies. Fifty years ago, famed economist Herbert Simon observed that because the human mind is poor at comprehending reality's complexity and dynamism, it relies on simple models to solve problems.[2] Such models are based heavily on experience and are the platform for intuition. The trouble is that reliance on mental models can limit or, worse, misguide cognition when humans are faced with unfamiliar and dynamic conditions, which aggravate complexity. This suggests that understanding global jihad–complex, unfamiliar and dynamic as it is—can be a huge challenge. Yet without that understanding, other aspects of COIN, namely, shaping conditions and conducting direct operations, cannot succeed.

Recognizing the jihad as an evolved form of insurgency is important. However, as Kilcullen, Mackinlay, and others have argued, it does not follow that the standard model of COIN is a satisfactory guide. In its classical form, COIN is optimized to prevent an insurgency from gaining control of a nation-state, not to counter a global movement that purports to defend Islam and Muslims everywhere and is disinterested in government as commonly defined. This difference is important not only because of the opportunities of global insurgency to move and hide in the seams of the world's nation-states but also because it confounds the standard model of COIN organization. That standard model, put forward by Robert Thompson 50 years ago, calls for integrating the political and military aspects into a holistic approach under a *single authority*—a "supremo"—so that, for example, uses of force do not undermine efforts to earn public support. However, in the absence of a global authority, it is far more difficult to integrate military strategies aimed at crushing insurgents with political strategies aimed at depriving them of the contested population's sympathy.[3]

The vast logical, geographic, and temporal distances between causes and effects in the jihad compound the difficulty of holistic management of COIN. A European government faced with rising Islamic radicalism has little chance of affecting U.S. techniques for interrogating jihadis in Guantanamo. The U.S. government battling jihadis on various fronts has even less chance of affecting European domestic policies that segregate, marginalize, and alienate Muslims. The Pakistani government's committment to help U.S. efforts to find bin Laden can be set back by the publication of cartoons in a Danish newspaper or the comments of the

---

[2] Gompert, Lachow, and Perkins (2005).

[3] Kilcullen (2005).

pope. The success of efforts by the U.S. military to stem the flow of jihadis from Syria into Iraq depends on how serious the Saudi government is about shutting off funding for that flow. Whole towns on Lebanon's Mediterranean coast are radicalized by veterans returning from fighting in Iraq.[4]

No "supremo" has the multinational authority, the multisectoral access, or the sheer omniscience to monitor and manage such linkages. Moreover, as this paper has already established, the way to respond to a decentralized and adaptable insurgency is by decentralizing COIN decisionmaking, not centralizing it. The puzzle of global COIN, then, is how to integrate its entire political-military effort, spanning the world, given the disutility and, in any case, impracticability of centralized authority.

Fortunately, information networking permits COIN to be both distributed *and* integrated by offering ways to provide access for anyone on the network to data anywhere on the network, as well as opportunities to collaborate horizontally without having to go through the hierarchy. This reinforces the need to invest in improved cognitive abilities up, down, and throughout the ranks of COIN, not just at headquarters.

Within this general approach to cognition—integration of intuition with reasoning, distributed throughout COIN—we can consider actual requirements. Using the framework for identifying needed capabilities for key aspects of COIN—understand, shape, and act—the role of cognitive capabilities is shown in Figure 6.1, with basic aspects of COIN along the top and types of capabilities down the side. Cognitive strengths are relevant to all key aspects of COIN and are highest in the stack of capabilities.

Recent work by the author and others has identified certain cognitive abilities as being particularly important in security operations because they create *time-information* advantages; that is, they use time to gain information, information to gain time, and the combination of time and information to gain operational advantage. These abilities are (1) anticipation, (2) opportunism, (3) decision speed, and (4) learning in action. In operations, these abilities are particularly valuable in achieving temporary advantage when the opposing sides are both networked, as is the case in global insurgency and global COIN.[5]

These abilities depend on a self-aware blending of experience-based intuition and information-based reasoning. They can be utilized effectively by employing what is known as *rapid-adaptive* decisionmaking techniques, in which intuition provides initial direction, creating time and access to information, expanding the opportunity to reason and to check and correct intuition, and so on—all done at speeds required by fast-breaking circumstances. The combination of these cognitive abilities and decisionmaking techniques is called *battle-wisdom*.

"Battle-wise" abilities offer operational benefits in networked conflict and are indispensable against adversaries that also possess them, as the Salafist jihad does. As noted, confining these abilities to senior ranks reduces their benefits. Distributed forces are most effective when not only information but also decisionmaking authority is distributed. In COIN, as in other irregular conflict, networked small units are often the best way to operate against

---

[4] Shadid (2006).

[5] Gompert, Lachow, and Perkins (2005).

Figure 6.1
COIN Requirements for Global Insurgency

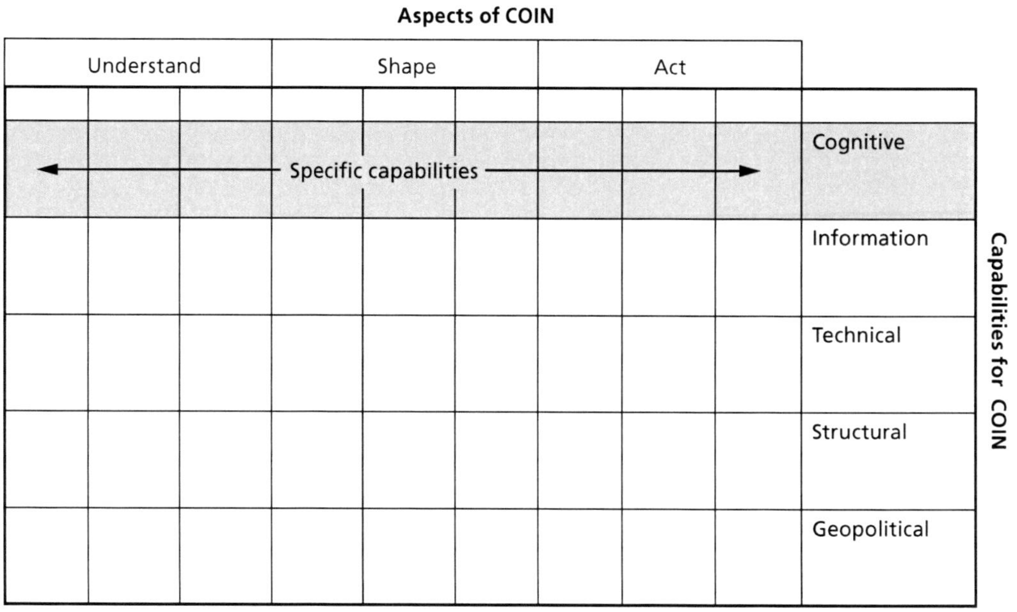

Aspects of COIN

Understand			Shape			Act			
									Cognitive
←			Specific capabilities					→	
									Information
									Technical
									Structural
									Geopolitical

Capabilities for COIN

RAND *OP168-6.1*

scattered enemies hiding in remote or densely populated areas. Success depends not only on the ability of such units to acquire and share information but also on how well and how fast they process it. This suggests, first, that small-unit leaders must have the authority to decide on their own and that they must be chosen and prepared to do so wisely. The need for battle-wisdom applies not only to military personnel but to all engaged in COIN operations, such as intelligence operatives, diplomats, spokespersons, law enforcers, and aid-givers.

There is a tendency to think that the people in COIN forces and agencies are already battle-wise, and many are to some extent. However, despite facing an adversary known to be both networked and clever, cognitive performance in networked operations has not been a high U.S. priority compared to the way other COIN resources have been developed and used, as noted earlier. Even with the advent of netcentric operations, U.S. COIN efforts remain preoccupied with structures and enamored with the technologies of force. Personnel systems and policies, including targeted recruitment and education, have been an afterthought, though this is beginning to change as the armed forces are reinvigorating COIN training in response to uneven performance in Iraq. That U.S. national security organizations have not even tried to define the particular cognitive abilities that are most important in countering global jihad, the chief current threat to national security, is a major omission.

DoD has described the operational challenges of counterterrorism as being able to *find, identify, track,* and *eliminate* terrorists.[6] Even this approach, while too narrow, implies formidable cognitive demands: Where will jihadis appear? Who is being recruited and motivated,

---

[6]   Joint Chiefs of Staff (2004).

and how? How can jihadis be distinguished from ordinary Muslims, or even from radical ones who may or may not be predisposed to violence? How can COIN operations possibly monitor the movement of all potential jihadis? How might their behavior facilitate finding and tracking them? How can jihadis be eliminated when their identities and whereabouts are uncertain and when more are recruited all the time? Given the risks of fanning the fires of insurgency, the challenges of finding, identifying, and tracking terrorists cannot be met by territorial control or by technology without effective brainwork.

Urgency is common in global COIN, whether in striking cells that have been disclosed, intercepting suicide attacks, or distinguishing nonviolent radical individuals from violent radical ones before using force. Because jihadists operate within larger populations and because non-jihadi casualties can substantiate the jihadist propaganda, decisions must be as careful as they are swift. Because of the mobility and suicide threat of jihadis, maximizing time-information is as important as it is difficult. With the right cognitive abilities, training, and decisionmaking methods, COIN troops and other agents can use information to gain time and use time to gain information, rather than sacrifice one for the other. In sum, effective COIN operations demand battle-wise actors able to make timely, informed, and thoughtful choices in the face of urgency and risk.

As for the analytical and shaping demands of COIN, there are critical questions that cannot be addressed adequately without exceptional cognitive powers: How can future forms and directions of the jihad be understood as it evolves—not in hindsight—given its complexity and its ability to adapt to changing conditions and countermeasures?[7] How can the beneficial processes and systems of globalization—trade, travel, common infrastructure, nongovernmental organizations, information flows—be managed vis-à-vis the opportunities they afford to global insurgency? How will political reform in Arab countries affect the jihad?

Both *understanding* jihad and *shaping* conditions to diminish its effectiveness and its effects depend on an appreciation of the jihadist personnel model described earlier. Since 2001, numerous events, actions, and statements in the name of the war on terrorism have poured fuel on the radicalization of Muslims and the expansion of the jihadist population. Some have resulted from deliberate policy, some from carelessness, and some from developments beyond the control of government. Some may have been essential despite their ramifications. The purpose here is not to open old wounds but instead to underscore the dynamics of global insurgency. That the strategic drawbacks of rough interrogation tactics were not foreseen is a deficiency of cognition, not just of morality. That the impact on Muslims' resentment of profiling "Middle Eastern–looking" men is not understood suggests that jihad itself is not undertstood.

Strategists are only now becoming attentive to the feedback loops whereby violent action may deepen resentment in the ummah, sustain the pool of jihadis, and perpetuate the Salafist insurgency. One encouraging sign is the growing number of articles in independent and military journals that go beyond bromides and offer serious analysis of global insurgency, of flawed

---

[7]   The global jihad has the attributes of a highly complex, dynamic, and adaptive system–the sort that has typically eluded unaided human cognition and simple explanatory models.

COIN, and of the need for wiser strategy. One hopes we are at the dawn of a period of realizing the deeper research, clearer reasoning, and blunter questioning that global COIN demands.

CHAPTER SEVEN

Cognitive Capabilities for COIN

Cognitive capabilities are similar to other capabilities in that requirements for them can be derived from missions and functions that must be performed to accomplish those missions. In the case of global COIN, the mission is to prevent a diffuse, intelligent, and vicious global insurgency from damaging the interests of the United States. The functions are to understand this insurgency, to shape the environment in which it lives, and to act directly against its capabilities and its violence. Properly defined, cognitive capabilities, like physical ones, can be developed and acquired through investment, tested, evaluated, tracked, and improved. Therefore, definition is important. What follows is an initial definition of cognitive capabilities needed for each of the main functions of global COIN.

Understanding Global Insurgency

The ingredients of understanding include

- collection of information
- sensitivity to factors that affect the behavior of the insurgency and the contested population
- interdisciplinary and international research and analysis
- vigorous debate, both in and out of government
- exposure of results to criticism.

Understanding is not a project but a process informed by constant contact with the environment. Jihad, like other insurgencies, changes with its environment, giving it an advantage over COIN, which changes by conscious policy. The aim of understanding is to reduce that advantage by keen awareness of the environment. In the effort to understand, the quest for consensus, consistency, and conformity must be subordinate to the quest for objectivity.

Anthony Cordesman has argued that "[W]ar fighters and officials who spin, lie, and exaggerate invariably do more than mislead others. The entire history of war shows that they end in lying to themselves. Such efforts to win support . . . overwhelm reality and the need to adapt and learn."[1] Because the jihad is more difficult than classical insurgency to comprehend

---

[1] Cordesman (2006b, pp. 3–4).

and counter on territorial and physical planes, there is a higher price to be paid for inadequacy, let alone self-deception, on the cognitive plane. Against an enemy that relies on a story of Islam under Western attack, the weight of COIN must shift from force to finesse.

Knowledge can never be complete or stable when it comes to complex and dynamic systems such as global insurgency. A massive and definitive new government study of the nature of global jihad is an especially bad idea if the findings are negotiated and, once approved, frozen. The formulaic tendency of U.S. national security bureaucracies to reduce subtle concepts and unstable phenomena to catchy acronyms obstructs thinking and stifles debate. Moreover, the U.S. government's questioning of assumptions behind policy can be inhibited by expectations of loyalty to political leadership, for whom a change of course may be taken as an admission of previous error. Against a cunning insurgency like al Qaeda, the effort to understand must be evidence-based, disciplined, transparent, objective, and free of the jargon and buzzwords of current policy. Risk-taking and iconoclasm should be promoted in policy, military, intelligence, and research communities. Self-awareness of possible bias and groupthink should be fostered.

The intelligence community's strict independence is imperative for successful COIN. Policymakers themselves should insist on nothing less. One of the advantages of having a Director of National Intelligence is the defense of independence he can mount at senior levels. Given the stakes in global COIN, if the executive branch cannot ensure such independence, Congress should.

Global COIN demands a commitment to vigorous and constant learning on the part of both practitioners and analysts. Every good analytic tool available should be used in such work: model-building, games, computer simulations, dialectic reasoning, hypothesis-testing, systems analysis, econometrics, and traditional scholarship. Evidence-based research and analytic methodology are real strengths of the United States and are more likely to aid understanding than televised heads are. Soldiers, intelligence analysts, and researchers should spend less time reading op-ed columns and more time pouring over serious literature and mining data.

The grist for analysis, from strategic to tactical, is reliable data. Empirical study is essential, lest anecdotes be used to support this or that contending opinion. Intelligence should be acquired by both "hunting" and "gathering" and should include direct and active personal observation. The government has acknowledged that there is no substitute for human intelligence (HUMINT) and that more is needed; yet, in Iraq, for example, U.S. troops patrolling in armored vehicles prevent it.[2] Global insurgents circulate far more easily among their enemies than COIN agents circulate among theirs. The inherent HUMINT advantage that jihad holds over COIN in Muslim populations cannot be eliminated, but it can be reduced. Covert spying will provide only a portion of the information needed to understand jihad. Much more will come from open sources and other activities. Every COIN actor should be a sensor.

U.S. and foreign analysis should be exchanged; better yet, joint U.S.-foreign analysis should be pursued. A way to guard against national myopia in understanding global insurgency is to perform international analysis. This requires overcoming any reluctance to weigh the views of foreign governments that may not accord with the current national line. U.S.

---

[2]   Alwyn-Foster (2005).

analysts and strategists should be attentive to foreign counterparts, not just try to convince them. Given the issue of Muslim communities in the Europe and North America, U.S.-EU channels would be excellent for international analysis, though of course inadequate in gaining non-Western perspectives.

To gain and maintain a deep understanding of global jihad, it is essential to comprehend how Muslims see their world, themselves, their religion, their values, and the West and its values. Strategic communications should involve more listening and less transmitting. Perceptions of injustice should be analyzed, not merely rebutted. Many if not most Muslims feel that they are underprivileged citizens of the world and are unsure where to turn to improve their lot. They lack political clout in Western countries, and in most Arab countries the only choice available is between acceptance of the regime and radical opposition. The failure of COIN strategists and practitioners to understand such frustration breeds "the erroneous assumption that given the justness of [COIN], actions [taken] in its name would be understood and accepted by the [Muslim] population."[3] As the final arbiter of the struggle between global jihad and global COIN, it would behoove us to learn more about this population. Unfortunately, many Western experts on the Muslim and Arab worlds are more intent on offering policy opinions than explaining why Muslims feel they are under attack.

The analytical campaign against jihad must be sensitive to indications of change in the characteristics and behavior of the insurgency as well as the effects of COIN. Understanding the cognitive patterns of martyrs, active jihadis, religious radicals, and mainstream Muslims must be sophisticated enough to support nuanced COIN strategies, words, and deeds. Such work must engage Muslims, including radicals and erstwhile jihadis. Interviews of detainees should aim to enrich the understanding of their milieu and mentality, not just extract leads.

Given the distributed nature of global insurgency and the limited time to act, small-unit actors on the front lines of COIN must have analytical skills and understanding of the sort just described. Global COIN cannot be linear, with analysis restricted to the worlds of intelligence and research; shaping done only by interagency committees and diplomats; and police, soldiers and intelligence agents expected only to carry out direct action. If COIN, more than warfare between sovereigns, demands understanding the effects of force, COIN against decentralized insurgency demands that that understanding be decentralized. A major faced with a decision to fire on a menacing crowd or on snipers holed up in a mosque must understand the potential impact of that choice on Muslim attitudes not only in that locale but worldwide. Checking with headquarters or Washington may be neither feasible nor advisable, since high command will have less appreciation of the immediate circumstances than the junior officer does.

In sum, data collection, evidenced-based analysis (interdisciplinary and international), sensitivity to the environment and the perceptions of Muslims, and distributed analytic ability are critical capabilities for understanding. For DoD, the effort to understand should concentrate on the ambiguities of force, especially how to use it against jihadist fighters, terrorists, and martyrs without confirming the story of Muslims and Islam under attack. The leadership at the Pentagon should insist that the military pursue *analytical COIN* with as much determination as it pursues forcible COIN.

---

[3]   Alwyn-Foster (2005, p. 6).

Global COIN-Shaping Strategy

The main difference between insurgency and interstate war is that the former involves a struggle for the support of more or less the same population, whereas each warring state has its own population.[4] Consequently, as stressed here and in classical COIN theory, the use of force by the governing power against the insurgency must take into account the likely impact on the sentiment of the population over which the struggle is being fought. So, too, must the insurgents be mindful of popular sentiment: Al-Zarqawi's killing of Sunni sheikhs who were willing to consider joining Iraq's political process appears to have crossed that line, to the advantage of COIN. However, in vying for popular support, the governing authority is at a disadvantage because the loss of *its* legitimacy to use force puts it on the same level as the insurgents—a victory for the latter.

COIN should aim to give the governing power a monopoly over the legitimate use of force, even if it cannot attain a monopoly over the ability to use force.[5] Against global insurgency, attacking the legitimacy of its use of force is at least as likely to bear fruit as is attacking the insurgency, especially if it is hidden in the ummah. The best chance for delegitimizing jihad lies in its own unrestrained, often suicidal violence against innocents and fellow Muslims. Imprecise COIN violence, indiscriminate arrest, and torture, on the other hand, can delegitimize the governing power and even legitimize the insurgency's violence. The contested population's standard of behavior for the governing power is, as it should be, higher than for jihad.

The quest for monopoly in the legitimate use of force is the essence of shaping and is largely cognitive. The side that is better at reading and affecting the attitude of the contested populace will tend to win, regardless of which side has more firepower. Data from Iraq are sobering. As of January 2006, 47 percent of Iraqis polled nationwide approve of attacks on U.S.-led forces. The number jumps to a chilling 88 percent among Iraq's Sunni Arabs. These numbers are worse from a U.S. standpoint than those of a year earlier, when 53 percent of Sunni Arabs polled considered "insurgent attacks [to be] a legitimate form of resistance." American COIN strategists can take some comfort in the fact that only 1 percent of Iraqis polled believe that attacks on Muslim civilians are justified, suggesting that ultra-extremist (*takfiri*) jihadis lose legitimacy by attacking Shiite pilgrims. But this also means that killing U.S. forces is much preferred over killing Iraqi civilians. Iraqis are equally united in their disapproval of the use of force by the U.S. military against Iraqi civilians. This means that every time civilians are killed by U.S. forces, COIN is considered to be no more legitimate than terrorism.[6] The data also suggest that U.S. occupation of Sunni lands gives legitimacy to attacks against U.S. forces, raising doubts about the value of territorial control.

---

[4]   Of course, nation-states at war, especially democratic ones, have to worry about the backing of their own populations and may try to break the enemy state's backing.

[5]   Kilcullen (2005).

[6]   Brookings Institution (2006, especially pp. 39–48).

Shaping must be geared toward meaningful objectives. Body counts and territorial control are neither useful goals nor reliable measures of progress in global COIN.[7] Strategy should be tailored according to effects on the security of Americans, their interests, and their ways of life, not according to traditional measures of warfare, e.g., victory, conquest, and surrender. Desired effects of global COIN include defusing (as opposed to waging and winning) worldwide religious war, keeping weapons of mass destruction (WMD) out of jihadist hands, preventing cataclysmic non-WMD attacks on U.S. and friendly soil, and maintaining market access to Middle East energy supplies. COIN shaping strategies should aim to have these desired effects by isolating violent Islamists, fostering genuine reform in Muslim-majority countries, reducing Muslim segregation in Western countries, and stigmatizing possession or use of WMD.

To the extent that shaping works, reliance on the use of force in COIN action can be reduced. Given the ambiguity of force in global COIN, one of the aims of smarter shaping is to use less force. By this reasoning, lower body counts may be a better indicator of progress than higher ones. High enemy body counts do not imply greater legitimacy in COIN force, or fewer enemies. Against the Salafist insurgency, killing may reinforce the jihadist story.

Because it is usually protracted, COIN has to contend with two political fronts: away and home. In shaping domestic support and confidence, understated resolve is better than stridency. The importance of words and tones of leaders and other spokespeople cannot be overstated, especially now that news is increasingly global and subject to misinterpretation or distortion. Against the global jihad, building bipartisan and coalition support is a critical duty of political leaders. As noted, however, arguments that are tempting for domestic use (e.g., branding Islamic radicalism, as such, as dangerous) could harm efforts to separate jihadis from nonviolent radicals. Information operations can be useful, but they are no substitute for educating COIN operatives at every level in how their words can help or harm the shaping strategy. In sum, global COIN capabilities must include well-turned communications by the few at the center as well as the many in the field.

Kilcullen has argued for a strategy of *disaggregating* the global insurgency, in that aggregating disparate Islamic movements and motives is both a strength and goal of al Qaeda.[8] Moreover, the more cohesive global jihad is, the harder it is for COIN to achieve the desired effects. Shaping should aim to break ties among the parts of jihad. However, because al Qaeda is so good at resonating with alienated Muslims, and because many Muslims feel that their community is threatened with injustice and violence, disaggregating is a huge cognitive challenge. Lumping all radical Islamists movements together as a single violent enemy may have a self-fulfilling effect. At every level, those involved in speaking for COIN must have the knowledge and vocabulary to weaken the links between global jihad and local insurgencies.

Of course, disaggregating involves not only communications but also substantive policy choices. Giving Sunnis a stake in Iraq's government should weaken cooperation between discontented Sunnis and irreconcilable jihadis (foreign and Iraqi). Reducing the involvement of U.S. troops in combat in Iraq would make it harder to depict U.S. support for the Iraqi state as part of a global war on Muslims. Progress toward an Israel-Palestine two-state solution would

---

[7] International Crisis Group (2006a).

[8] Kilcullen (2005).

set back Salafist hopes of drawing Hamas supporters into global jihad. Autonomy for Thailand's Patani province could frustrate jihadist intensification of that conflict. The point here is not to argue the pros and cons of such policies but to remind that cognitive shaping in COIN must address larger agendas. At a minimum, the U.S. government should inventory all the policies that may cause its "global war on terrorism" to appear to be a global war on Islam.

Shaping is largely about discrediting the narrative of the adversary in the eyes of the contested population. Again, this is hard when many Muslims believe that they are the targets of attack because of who they are. Whatever the merits of these beliefs, they are deeply rooted in Western dominance and Muslim disappointment of history since the Ottoman collapse of 1918, if not longer. A prerequisite for effective shaping is this understanding. In turn, the combination of improved understanding and shaping can reduce the need for force and increase the legitimacy of force—and thus discredit the jihadist story and disrupt the jihadist regenerative "personnel model." Such a high return on investment in understanding and shaping underscores the importance of shifting U.S. COIN priorities.

Global COIN Operations

Nothing in this paper should be read to mean that direct, lethal operations against global jihad must be avoided. Even if Muslim anger is justifiable, it hardly justifies the wanton savagery that characterizes the jihad. The United States has to protect itself and others in need of its protection. Even if using force against jihadis does not reduce their ranks, it may curb their killing. The challenge is to conduct security operations so that the jihad will be weakened rather than strengthened—at its heart, a challenge of cognition.

The difficulty of making judgments on the use of force in the midst of a contested population is recognized in classical COIN. However, this difficulty is even more acute in the case of COIN against the global Salafist insurgency for two reasons: the danger of confirming the jihadist story that Islam is under attack and the jihadis' own pattern of violence.

As noted, to rid the Muslim world of Western power and control, the jihad calls for counteroffensive measures in the West. This insurgent strategy presents two different cases regarding U.S. or allied use of military force:

- In Muslim-majority countries, the use of Western military power is the reason given by jihadis for Muslims to counterattack in the West; therefore, it must be carefully metered with this effect in mind.
- As such counterattacks occur in Western Muslim-minority countries, the use of Western military power must yield to law enforcement because of strong and important norms against domestic use of military forces.

In both cases, the United States and its allies must exercise great restraint in the use of force against an insurgency whose fighters, being duty-bound to defend Islam, resort to unrestrained, suicidal violence in order to produce maximum death and shock. Thus, paradoxically, while the United States enjoys a huge advantage over the global insurgency in the capacity for force, it is at a huge disadvantage in its freedom to use it. *If follows that thinking and decisionmaking about the use of instruments of force are, if anything, more important than the capabilities of those instruments.*

As noted, shaping strategy should be informed by judgments on how to reduce reliance on the use of force and how to gain a monopoly in the legitimate use of force. Beyond this, when undertaking actual operations, COIN security forces themselves require the ability to make sound judgments regarding when, where, against whom, to what end, by whom, with what means, and at what level to resort to violence. While some general rules can be set—minimize noncombatant casualties, for instance—the fluidity and complexity of global insurgency and the corresponding need for flexibility argue against complete reliance on written manuals. The distribution of information, cognitive abilities, and decisionmaking authority must permit sound judgments to be made in action, with no time to spare, by those on the front lines of COIN.

This returns us to the *time-information* challenge described earlier, perhaps the most important challenge on the cognitive plane of COIN operations. In COIN, if anything is as vital as information, it is time. In the classical view, time and information are in tension: By the time all relevant information is acquired, the moment for effective action has passed; conversely, timely action may be less than effective because it is not sufficiently well informed. The network revolution changes this. Of course, distributed information cannot actually slow the passage of time, but it can enhance the product of time and information (i.e., time *times* information). In operational decisionmaking, the immediate availability of credible and useful information can make time more productive and compensate for a lack of time—in effect, make time "last longer."

Again, the more complex, fluid, and unfamiliar operational conditions are—and global COIN surely fits that description—the greater the need to balance and blend intuition with reasoning. Although the quickening tempo of conflict can, in effect, compress time available for reasoning, information networking can, as just explained, decompress time. This can increase the opportunity for and improve the quality of reasoning, thereby enhancing operational performance, especially as it relates to the use of force.

The concept of time-information can be explained another way. The quality of an operational decision should improve as a function of both time and information. With the right sort of decisionmaking—the rapid-adaptive decisionmaking explained earlier—time and information can have a strong positive correlation: the more time, the greater the chance to acquire more information; the more information, the more effectively time can be used. Although the time available to operational decisionmakers in COIN may be declining due to higher operating tempo, the availability of abundant useful information, thanks to networking, can compensate for this. Up to a point, information networking can conserve or create time otherwise consumed by chasing, gathering, and sifting through data. In sum, networking can aid operational decisionmaking by enhancing time-information capabilities, permitting reasoning and improving cognition despite urgency.[9]

---

[9] Gompert, Lachow, and Perkins (2005).

At present, COIN is at a time-information *dis*advantage relative to the jihad. U.S. COIN agents are slow or hesitant to act when not in possession of complete information; yet hasty action can produce results that aid the jihadis, such as civilian casualties. Closing this time-information gap demands improved sense-making and decisionmaking in operations, not just better IT. After all, COIN already has use of better IT systems than the jihadis do, and yet the operational advantage all too often lies with the latter.

It is striking how little U.S. operating elements (e.g., troops, intelligence agents, police, diplomats) have benefited from the revolution in "user-reach" information networking that is sweeping the world outside of national security.[10] Those on the front lines of COIN are operating in an information environment that is sluggish, congested, and unresponsive relative to what the typical Internet-using traveler, shopper, or investor has today, and relative to the needs of 21st-century COIN. For a soldier or official in need of information relevant to a specific COIN situation, data does not travel at light speed but rather at bureaucratic speed because it has to cross organizational, security, and network-control boundaries where it is slowed. In COIN and other security operations, the possibilities of user-reach remain blocked by the culture of need-to-know. Information sharing and integration are often subordinated to information denial and compartmentalization.

Ignoring the remarkable leverage provided in recent years by user-reach (or search) technology in other sectors, intelligence and military headquarters and bureaucracies still insist on "processing" information–sifting, sorting, analyzing, validating, sanitizing, and otherwise massaging it–before posting it for users to use. The processors, not the users, decide what processing is appropriate. They also decide which users can be trusted with the information. Whatever value such processing and control add is at the expense of timely access and collaboration by COIN operators and users. The net effect of failing to catch the latest wave in the information revolution is nothing less than the forfeiture of the time-information advantage. Cognitive superiority in direct COIN operations will be elusive as long as the government fails to provide its users unobstructed information access and unhindered collaboration.

Better exploitation of search and collaborative technologies is necessary but not sufficient.[11] Better thinking and problem-solving during operations are also needed. As noted earlier, the ability of operational decisionmakers to integrate reliable intuition with speedy reasoning is essential in COIN situations that are unfamiliar, complex, and urgent. In selecting and developing people for COIN operations, the military and other organizations should emphasize the ability to anticipate, recognize, and exploit opportunities; make quick decisions that create rather than foreclose options; and learn in action, as well as the self-awareness that characterizes good problem-solvers. The importance of horizontal sharing and collaboration in COIN operations, with or without prior plans, makes it essential to revise command-and-control schemes so that hierarchical dependence, prerogative, and interference are minimized.

COIN operations could be improved by understanding and addressing the forms of networking that characterize the global insurgency. As mentioned earlier, recent work at RAND reveals the significance of jihadist "nodes, hubs, and cores," the first being fighters, terrorists,

---

[10] This is documented and diagnosed in Gompert, Barry, and Andreassen (2006).

[11] Future RAND research will examine the problem of user reach in COIN in greater depth.

and other operatives; the second being the tier responsible for planning, financial operations, communications, material support, and providing direction to the nodes; and the third being the theoreticians and charismatic leaders.[12] While a great deal of attention has been given to nodes and cores, this ongoing RAND work highlights the advantage of targeting *hubs*—the middle tiers that are critical to enabling nodes to turn the ideological guidance of the cores into action. Such hubs can be neutralized by physical, electronic, financial, legal, intelligence, or political means. The selection of such targets and means is crucial and difficult, and it must remain a human cognitive function instead of an automated or prescripted one, given the agility of the adversary and the ambiguity of the use of force in COIN.

In line with the aim of disaggregating global insurgency, severing links between global and local components, and between hubs and nodes, is also important. Whatever means are used to do the severing, the key is to understand the links. This requires better analysis and then translating analysis into concepts of operation. Dividing the enemy is an idea as old as warfare. The argument for it in global COIN is compelling, and it must be attempted both strategically and tactically, both tangibly and cognitively.

At the same time, a strategy of disaggregation should not breed complacency about the ideological power of the core. The "energy source" of the jihadist network, again, is the ability to resonate, recruit, and regenerate by legitimizing terrorism and martyrdom in defense of an embattled Muslim community and Islamic faith. This, too, is increasingly distributed. It would be a fallacy to equate it with a single point. The Salafist insurgency has spread beyond the point at which taking out its center will eliminate its cognitive energy.

Thus, the ability of the jihad to perpetuate itself is no longer concentrated, which means it is less vulnerable to physical annihilation. This brings us back to the need for cognitive effectiveness and the imperative of wresting legitimacy from the insurgency in direct COIN operations no less than in strategy and pronouncements. Because of the jihadis' skill in manipulating and amplifying news through global media, actions will have more impact than will words on the legitimacy of both COIN and insurgency. It has already been stressed that action cannot be calibrated and conducted by capitals and headquarters without an unacceptable loss of operational speed and responsiveness. This means that the ability to understand the effects of actions on legitimacy must be distributed and enhanced throughout the operating ranks of COIN, as already noted. When innocent people are killed in a COIN strike, when prisoners are abused, when towns in which terrorists hide are devastated, the failure is one of insufficient understanding of the importance of legitimacy in COIN compared to state-to-state warfare. The agents of COIN must be educated to know that the attitude of the population observing them and feeling the effects of their actions is the prize of the larger contest.

The culture of the U.S. military is oriented toward lethal operations. A British veteran of recent operations in Iraq has noted that the U.S. Army is too inclined toward offensive operations, as if killing insurgents is the strategic objective.[13] Given jihadis' methods, the number of them needed to cause death and destruction worldwide is small. Moreover, strategy and actions aimed at reducing their numbers overlooks that the real problems are the fanaticism

---

[12] Brennan et al. (2005).

[13] Alwyn-Foster (2005).

of the jihadis and their ability to refill ranks, both of which may increase in response to U.S. military action. Neither the size nor the intensity of the insurgency in Iraq has been diminished by killing and detaining insurgents. Indeed, perceived indiscriminate detention in Sunni areas helped reinvigorate the insurgency in the first year of the occupation. The consequences of running up body counts and conducting suspect sweeps must inform the reasoning and decisionmaking on which direct COIN action is based.

In addition to the problem of the U.S. military's culture of lethality are the can-do attitude and sense of moral rectitude of the U.S. military, both of which impede self-criticism and self-improvement. To its credit, the military is becoming increasingly introspective, owing to frustration over operating results in Iraq and Afghanistan. Recent initiatives to learn and conduct smarter COIN and the appearance of critical papers by military officers and retirees are constructive developments. Particularly noteworthy are the U.S. military's COIN training initiatives in Iraq and at the Army's Command and General Staff College. These initiatives amount to a healthy admission that global COIN must be smarter.

COIN operations are not limited to the use of force. Intelligence operations can be at least as important as violent military operations while also making military operations less violent, more legitimate, and more effective. With the advent of precision weapons, acquiring the intelligence needed to find the right targets at the right time and right place is more difficult and critical than the actual attack, as the elimination of al-Zarqawi so graphically showed. After a steady romance with technical collection that began early in the Cold War, the U.S. intelligence community is coming around to the recognition that the essence of good intelligence is cognition: not just human collection but human understanding. The special importance of intelligence operations in COIN lies in the fact that the use of force can backfire unless carefully calibrated. It may be better not to use force than to use it in a way that will confirm the jihadist story of Muslims under attack. Force without intelligence—in both senses of intelligence—is a ticket to failure in COIN.[14]

So far, we have dealt only with U.S. cognitive capabilities for COIN. In addition, the United States has a huge stake in improving its partners' ability to understand, shape, and act. This does not mean that U.S. COIN personnel should proceed as if they have superiority on this plane. Indeed, there is much to learn from others. In the words of U.S. Under Secretary of Defense Eric Edelman, "In many cases, coalition partners will be better able to deal with [jihad] because they know the culture, the geography, and the language in which [it is] operating."[15] In seeking to build the capacity of local allies for effective COIN, the United States should place as much stress on its ability to make sound judgments, especially regarding the use of force, as it does on increasing its firepower.

Prior to outlining investments needed to outsmart jihad, it is useful to sum up key cognitive capabilities. Figure 7.1 places various cognitive capabilities across the main priorities of COIN. (Because capabilities on the cognitive layer rely on the information layer, the figure

---

[14] The success of the Turkish government in curbing the growth and operations of the Islamist radical group Turkish Hizballah lies in a series of "intelligence coups" (Nugent, 2004).

[15] Quoted in Garamone (2006).

also summarizes key IT and information-management capabilities even though these are to be explored in a separate forthcoming RAND study.) This summary is by no means comprehensive or adequately detailed; it is just a start.

Figure 7.1
COIN Requirements for Global Insurgency

Aspects of COIN

Understand			Shape			Act			
Information gathering	Objective interdisciplinary, international analysis	Contact with jihad and contested population	Reduce and legitimize use of force	Delegiti-mize jihadist violence	Measure by effects (not by attrition)	Reliable intuition and timely reasoning	Rapid-adaptive decision making	Distributed decision authority	**Cognitive**
Open-source sorting	ISR	HUMINT	Hearing insurgent	Hearing friends	Education reform	Fast data fusion	Information user primacy	Unobstructed horizontal collaboration	**Information**
									Technical
									Structural
									Geopolitical

Capabilities for COIN

NOTE: ISR = intelligence, surveillance, and reconnaissance.

RAND OP168-7.1

CHAPTER EIGHT

Conclusions: Investment and Reform

It would be untrue to say that the U.S. national security establishment is neglecting altogether the cognitive requirements for understanding, shaping, and operating in COIN, just as it would be unfair to suggest that the people involved in COIN possess none of the right abilities. The question at hand is whether doing more in this domain would be a good investment. The combination of the shrewdness of the global Salafist insurgency, the opportunity afforded—to both sides—by information networking, and the low priority presently given to the cognitive domain suggests a need to identify, prioritize, and invest in strengthening U.S. abilities to reason and decide under the theme of "outsmarting jihad."

Investment in cognitive capabilities should encompass personnel policy, training and education, research and analysis, command-and-control transformation, and other measures of potential and enduring value. As an overall theme, given that global insurgency is a matter of unsurpassed concern to the United States, the needs of global COIN should figure centrally in the development and employment of human resources in national security services and agencies.

Several investments and other measures should be considered:

- *Profiles and standards* for cognitive excellence in personnel for analytical and operational COIN functions should be devised and applied in recruitment, advancement, assignment, development, and retention. Priority should be given to these needs in the allocation of resources for personnel.
- The U.S. government should gear up for vigorous *competition* with the private economy to attract people matching the profiles and meeting the standards associated with excellence in COIN. It is no coincidence that many of the cognitive abilities needed for COIN are increasingly valued in markets. This means that the U.S. economy will produce people with many of the right attributes, but it is up to the government to recruit and keep them.
- *Personnel policies* should be tailored specifically to meet needs for improved cognitive effectiveness in COIN:
  - Recruitment goals, strategies, and resources should be aligned with COIN requirements.
  - Performance evaluation, advancement, and assignment standards and policies should favor these same needs.

 – Retention strategies, including compensation levels, other incentives, and career management should be tailored to meet COIN needs.
- Professional *education and training* for the military, intelligence, law enforcement, and diplomatic services should be oriented to prepare people for the sorts of cognitive challenges that arise in COIN:
    – Curricula should stress reasoning in understanding, shaping, and operations, including making judgments about the use of force, not simply acquiring information.
    – Nongovernmental education opportunities should be expanded and rewarded, thus combating tendencies toward groupthink and conformity with policy.
    – In both government and nongovernment educational settings, individuals should be given incentives to do serious research and analysis of insurgency and COIN.
    – Training techniques should be developed and used to integrate intuition and reasoning, to heighten self-awareness, and to foster adaptive decisionmaking under stress, urgency, and uncertainty.
- The power and prerogatives of *information users* should be made a priority in IT networks and applications for COIN. To this end, help from leaders of the Internet-based smart-user revolution should be sought to help overcome barriers to information access and collaboration.
- Command-and-control systems and culture should be transformed to *decentralize decisionmaking authority* for COIN (and, for that matter, for military operations of all sorts).

Analysis of investments of these sorts, including their costs and other implications, can and should be taken to deeper levels than those just sketched. A useful methodology in such analysis is to determine where the next dollar for COIN capabilities could most profitably go. To illustrate, consider what should be done specifically to improve operational decisionmaking when recruiting military personnel with the battle-wise abilities of particular utility in COIN described earlier. One measure is lateral entry, i.e., recruiting individuals who have already exhibited key cognitive capabilities in occupations analogous to COIN (e.g., criminal police work or emergency medical response). Another is to direct entry-level recruitment resources and messages toward relevant cognitive profiles and standards. A third is to undertake compensation reform to attract and keep individuals with exceptional and needed cognitive capabilities. This is illustrated in Figure 8.1.

Similar investment paths can and should be developed for all important cognitive capabilities—interdisciplinary and international analysis for better understanding, measures to strengthen user reach in information access and collaboration, education and training on decisions regarding use of force, and so on. Then, priority should be placed on those investments with the greatest return, based on the criticality of their contribution to COIN and their cost-effectiveness.

Appended to this paper is a more comprehensive, though still preliminary, outline of investments and other measures to enhance cognitive capabilities for COIN.

Figure 8.1
DoD Investment Priorities for Global COIN

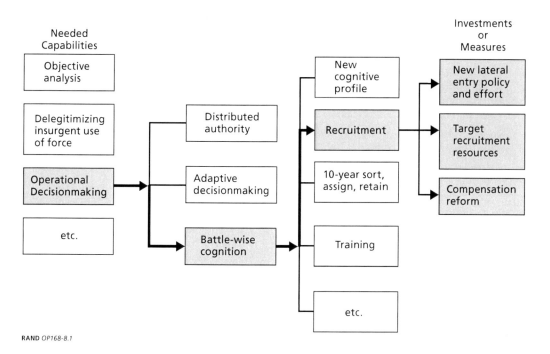

RAND *OP168-8.1*

Specific measures could be taken without delay to strengthen cognitive capabilities for COIN. For instance,

- reaching out to conduct international analysis of the changing global insurgency and how to shape conditions to reduce and legitimize the use of force against it
- training and education on how and why some members of the Muslim community travel the path to militancy, violence, and martyrdom, taking into account Islamic attitudes, ideals, and grievances, as well as the effects of the use of force on these phenomena
- direct involvement of the personnel departments of military, intelligence, law enforcement, and other national security organizations in COIN capability-building strategies.

Global COIN is as challenging as it is because the complexities and ambiguities of traditional COIN are compounded by the globalization of insurgent motivations, means, and communications; the de-territorialization of operations; and religious extremism. Overcoming this challenge requires not only specific investments such as those just suggested, but also the creation of institutional conditions that favor objective and sophisticated cognition.

A growing number of credible voices have flagged institutional conditions that are *not* conducive to smarter COIN. For example, U.S. officers in Iraq "rarely if ever questioned authority, and were reluctant to deviate from precise instructions. Staunch loyalty upward and conformity to one's superior were noticeable traits." Low-level initiative was discouraged.[1] "The

---

[1] Alwyn-Foster (2005, p. 6).

culture of the U.S. Army does not encourage rapid response to changing situations." There is a belief in U.S. military and official circles that the country is either at war or at peace, rather than at something in between.[2] Such observations imply that prescriptions for investment in cognitive capabilities for global COIN may fall on institutional deaf ears. Therefore, as a complement to specific measures, institutional cultures—military, intelligence, law enforcement, foreign service—should be reformed so that people who want to question conventional wisdom, are willing to take intellectual and political risk, and are aware of the need to use force wisely are given encouragement and responsibility.

Leaders of the agencies and services responsible for COIN must signal their determination to put more brainpower into the mission. It is their job to create space within the military and the intelligence community for questioning conventional analysis of jihad, and to support unfettered research, analysis, and debate. They must also move personnel policy and development to the center of strategy. A general lesson of the information revolution is that it is essential, sooner rather than later, to turn attention from technology to people. Generally speaking, human-resource policies and investments in the U.S. government do not reflect the priority that has been placed on countering global insurgency, much less the increased cognitive effectiveness that is essential. However, before senior officials state a commitment to enhancing the role and quality of thinking and decisionmaking in COIN, they must be sure that their statements will be backed by resources and will lead to action.

Internally driven reform will not be enough. After all, military and civilian bureaucracies will not find it easy to seek and use cognitive skills that are uncommon in those very bureaucracies. Frank and objective external analysis is needed, from unbiased research organizations, analogous sectors, other countries, and Muslims of all schools of thought, even from ex-jihadis. Because of vested interests in the ways the government manages its people and how they think, it would be useful to get an unconstrained, outside look at how well it measures up to the cognitive demands of global COIN and what it can do to improve.

It should be a source of discomfort that jihadist leaders place greater emphasis on human capital—intellectuals, motivators, planners, information technicians, and operating agents—for holy war than the United States does for COIN. To some extent, this a reflection of the many other advantages (e.g., firepower) the United States has over the insurgents. But those other advantages will do little good, and possible some harm, if not coupled with better thinking.

The jihad has crafted a powerful story to justify terrorism as self-defense of the weak. It also has a proven ability to mobilize and expend people who combine ingenuity with religious fury. Its ability of self-perpetuation is no longer concentrated in one leader, one place, one country. Yet global COIN operatives have acted as if the ability to produce (and reproduce) martyrs can be crushed by force. The insurgency's excellence in the cognitive and spiritual domains means that COIN operations must shift their emphasis toward people and minds. The United States is brimming with brainpower. It will need to assemble it more ambitiously, hone it more sharply, and employ it more purposefully to counter this threat.

---

[2] Nagl (2005).

Investments and Measures to Enhance Cognitive COIN Capabilities

Table A.1
Cognitive Capabilities and Required Measures and Investments

	Needed Cognitive Capabilities	Existing or Programmed Capabilities	Steps Required to Fill Gaps
Understanding	Objective research	Subjective; constrained by current policy; politicized	Reward and protect objectivity; promote external independent analysis
	Advanced analytic tools	COIN not attracting or exploiting cutting-edge tools	Challenge federally funded research and development centers to apply tools to COIN
	Continuous close contact with environment	Inconsistent; not systematic	Dedicate resources
	Contact with insurgents	Not exploiting detainees or defectors to deepen understanding	Create program to learn from detainees
	International analysis	Little or none under government auspices	Launch programs through NATO and other countries
	Unconventional and innovative thinking	Beginning to occur in military; stress is on standard doctrine	Reward people and ideas that challenge status quo
	Superior analytical skills in military	Not consistently stressed or measured	Establish standards and metrics; create incentives
	Superior analytical skills in intelligence	Intelligence community not competitive for superior analytic skills	Improve recruitment and retention
	Superior analytical ability of local friends	Largely ignored	Introduce as objective of security-sector reform
	Distributed understanding	Minimal effort	Preoperation orientation and learning during operations

Table A.1—Continued

	Needed Cognitive Capabilities	Existing or Programmed Capabilities	Steps Required to Fill Gaps
Shaping	Legitimize U.S. and host-government forces	Addressed in new COIN manual	Inculcate in every operator
	Delegitimize insurgent forces	Left to information operations and spokespeople	Inculcate in every operator
	Isolate insurgents	Left to information operations and spokespeople	Inculcate in every operator
	Address material needs of population	Inconsistent; top-down	Provide operators with awareness and tools
	Address political needs of population	Inconsistent; top-down	Provide operators with awareness and tools
	Strengthen legitimacy of targeted government	Inconsistent; top-down	Provide operators with awareness and tools
	Disrupt insurgent recruiting process	Minimal effort	Familiarize operators with problem
Acting	All operators understand civil-military strategy	Ad hoc and uneven	Preoperation training and screening
	Awareness of risks and benefits of force	Ad hoc and uneven	Develop programs to ensure
	Decentralized decisionmaking authority	Command-and-control reform in infancy	Radical revision of traditional command-and-control doctrine to exploit information
	User primacy for data access	Need-to-know culture and rules still dominant	Revise network access
	Unobstructed horizontal collaboration	Informal and tentative	Develop protocols and tools
	Rapid-adaptive decisionmaking	Not formally trained or employed	Develop training
	Superior intuitive and rational-choice abilities	Not an explicit priority	Create curricula to teach; learn from other sectors; lateral recruitment
	Initiative, opportunism, anticipation	No standards	Set standards
	Ability to learn in action	Ad hoc	Systematic study

Bibliography

Alberts, David S., and Richard E. Hayes, *Power to the Edge: Command . . . Control . . . in the Information Age*, Command and Control Research Program, 2003. Online at http://www.dodccrp.org/publications/pdf/Alberts_Power.pdf (as of September 11, 2006).

"Al Qaeda's Fatwa," English translation of February 23, 1998, fatwa signed by Osama bin Laden and Ayman al-Zawahiri, *NewsHour with Jim Lehrer*, undated. Online at http://www.pbs.org/newshour/terrorism/international/fatwa_1998.html (as of September 27, 2006).

Alwyn-Foster, Nigel, "Changing the Army for Counterinsurgency Operations," *Military Review*, November–December 2005, pp. 2–15. Online at http://usacac.army.mil/CAC/milreview/download/English/NovDec05/aylwin.pdf (as of September 12, 2006).

Barno, David W., "Challenges in Fighting a Global Insurgency," *Parameters, U.S. Army War College Quarterly*, Vol. 36, No. 2, Summer 2006, pp. 15–29. Online at http://www.carlisle.army.mil/USAWC/Parameters/06summer/barno.pdf (as of September 11, 2006).

Benjamin, Daniel, and Steven Simon. "Zarqawi's Life After Death," *New York Times*, June 9, 2006, p. A27.

bin Laden, Osama, Captured Letter to Mullah Mohammed Omar, undated. English translation available through West Point Combating Terrorism Center, online at http://www.ctc.usma.edu/aq/AFGP-2002-600321-Trans.pdf (as of September 11, 2006).

Bird, Kai, and Martin J. Sherwin, *American Prometheus: The Triumph and Tragedy of J. Robert Oppenheimer*, New York: Knopf, 2005.

Brennan, Richard, Adam Grissom, Sara A. Daly, Peter Chalk, William Rosenau, Kalev Sepp, and Stephen Dalzell, "Future Insurgency Threats," unpublished RAND research, 2005.

Brookings Institution, *Iraq Index: Tracking Variables of Reconstruction and Security in Post-Saddam Iraq*, Washington, D.C., March 30, 2006. Online at http://www.brookings.edu/fp/saban/iraq/index20060330.pdf (as of April 3, 2006).

Celeski, Joseph D., *Operationalizing COIN*, JSOU Report 05-2, Hurlburt Field, Fla.: Joint Special Operations University Press, 2005.

Cohen, Eliot, Conrad Crane, Jan Horvath, and John Nagl, "Principles, Imperatives, and Paradoxes of Counterinsurgency," *Military Review*, March–April 2006, pp. 49–53. Online at http://usacac.leavenworth.army.mil/CAC/milreview/English/MarApr06/Cohen.pdf (as of September 11, 2006).

Coll, Steve, "Citizens," *New Yorker*, June 5, 2006. Online at http://www.newyorker.com/talk/content/articles/060605ta_talk_coll (as of August 2, 2006).

Cordesman, Anthony H., *The Iraq War and Its Lessons for Counterinsurgency*, Washington, D.C.: Center for Strategic International Studies Press, 2005.

———, "Give the Defense Department an F," *Los Angeles Times*, June 3, 2006a). Online at http://www.latimes.com/news/opinion/commentary/la-oe-cordesman3jun03,0,837411.story?coll=la-news-comment-opinions (as of June 9, 2006).

———, "Measuring Security and Stability in Iraq: The August 2006 Quarterly Report: Progress but Far from the Facts the Nation Needs and Deserves," working draft, Washington, D.C.: Center for Strategic and International Studies, September 5, 2006b. Online at http://www.csis.org/media/csis/pubs/060905_iraq_quarterly.pdf (as of September 20, 2006).

Council on American-Islamic Relations, "U.S. Muslim Religious Council Issues Fatwa Against Terrorism," July 27, 2005. Online at http://www.cair-net.org/downloads/fatwa.htm (as of September 12, 2006).

Devji, Faisal, *Landscapes of the Jihad*, Ithaca, N.Y.: Cornell University Press, 2005.

Director, Office of Force Transformation, Office of the Secretary of Defense, "Network-Centric Warfare: Creating a Decisive Warfighting Advantage," Washington, D.C.: U.S. Department of Defense, Winter 2003. Online at http://www.oft.osd.mil/library/library_files/document_318_NCW_GateFold-Pages.pdf (as of September 20, 2006).

DoD—*see* U.S. Department of Defense.

Garamone, Jim, "Terrorists Will Test American Resolve, DoD Policy Official Says," *American Forces Information Service*, March 30, 2006. Online at http://www.defenselink.mil/news/Mar2006/20060330_4662.html (as of June 19, 2006).

Gompert, David C., Charles L. Barry, and Alf A. Andreassen, *Extending the User's Reach: Responsive Networking for Integrated Military Operations*, Washington, D.C.: National Defense University, Center for Technology and National Security Policy, February 2006. Online at http://www.ndu.edu/ctnsp/Def_Tech/DTP%2024%20Extending%20User%20Reach.pdf (as of September 11, 2006).

Gompert, David C., Irving Lachow, and Justin Perkins, *Battle-Wise: Gaining Advantage in Networked Warfare*, Washington, D.C.: National Defense University, Center for Technology and National Security Policy, January 2005. Online at http://www.ndu.edu/ctnsp/Def_Tech/DTP8%20Battlewise.pdf (as of September 11, 2006).

Gunaratna, Rohan, *Inside Al Qaeda: Global Network of Terror*, New York: Columbia University Press, 2002.

Hafez, Mohammed M., "Jihadi Salafism and Justifications for Suicide Terrorism," briefing, RAND Corporation, Arlington, Va., January 11, 2006.

Hamas, "Hamas Covenant 1988: The Covenant of the Islamic Resistance Movement," August 18, 1988. Online at http://www.yale.edu/lawweb/avalon/mideast/hamas.htm (as of September 11, 2006).

Hoffman, Bruce, "Does Our Counter-Terrorism Strategy Match the Threat?" testimony presented before the House International Relations Committee, Subcommittee on International Terrorism and Nonproliferation, Santa Monica, Calif.: RAND Corporation, CT-250-1, 2005. Online at http://www.rand.org/pubs/testimonies/CT250-1/ (as of September 12, 2006).

Ignatius, David, "Fighting Smarter in Iraq," *Washington Post*, March 17, 2006, p. A19. Online at http://www.washingtonpost.com/wp-dyn/content/article/2006/03/16/AR2006031601308.html (as of September 11, 2006).

International Crisis Group, *In Their Own Words: Reading the Iraqi Insurgency*, Amman and Brussels, February 15, 2006a.

————, *The Next Iraqi War? Sectarianism and Civil Conflict*, Amman, Baghdad, and Brussels, February 27, 2006b.

Joint Chiefs of Staff, *The National Military Strategy of the United States of America*, 2004. Online at http://www.defenselink.mil/news/Mar2005/d20050318nms.pdf (as of April 4, 2006).

Kilcullen, David J., "Countering Global Insurgency," *Journal of Strategic Studies*, Vol. 28, No. 4, August 2005, pp. 597–615.

Kissinger, Henry A., "After Lebanon," Tribune Media Services, September 13, 2006. Online at http://www.tmsfeatures.com/tmsfeatures/subcategory.jsp?custid=67&catid=1592 (as of September 21, 2006).

Mackinlay, John, "Defeating Complex Insurgency: Beyond Iraq and Afghanistan," London: Royal United Services Institute, 2005.

Mackinlay, John, and Alison Al-Baddawy, "Rethinking Counterinsurgency," Santa Monica, Calif.: RAND Corporation, OP-177-OSD, forthcoming.

Miller, John, Transcript of interview with Osama bin Laden, May 1998. Online at http://www.pbs.org/wgbh/pages/frontline/shows/binladen/who/interview.html (as of June 16, 2006).

Moore, Jeff, "Islamic Insurgency Run Amok," *Proceedings* [U.S. Naval Institute], Vol. 132, No. 4, May 2006, pp. 38–43.

Nagl, John, *Learning to Eat Soup with a Knife: Counterinsurgency Lessons from Malaya and Vietnam*, Chicago, Ill.: University of Chicago Press, 2005.

Negroponte, John D., *Annual Threat Assessment of the Director of National Intelligence for the Senate Select Committee on Intelligence*, Washington, D.C., February 2, 2006. Online at http://intelligence.senate.gov/0602hrg/060202/negroponte.pdf (as of September 11, 2006).

Nugent, John T., Jr., "The Defeat of Turkish Hizballah as a Model for Counter-Terrorism Strategy," *Middle East Review of International Affairs*, Vol. 8, No. 1, March 2004, pp. 69–76. Online at http://meria.idc.ac.il/journal/2004/issue1/jv8n1a6.html (as of June 9, 2006).

Packer, George, "The Lesson of Tal Afar: Is It Too Late for the Administration to Correct Its Course in Iraq?" The New Yorker, April 10, 2006, pp. 48–65. Online at http://www.newyorker.com/fact/content/articles/060410fa_fact2 (as of September 12, 2006).

Pape, Robert A., *Dying to Win: The Strategic Logic of Suicide Terrorism*, New York: Random House, 2005.

Petraeus, David H., "Learning Counterinsurgency: Observations from Soldiering in Iraq," *Military Review*, January–February 2006, pp. 2–12. Online at http://usacac.leavenworth.army.mil/CAC/milreview/English/JanFeb06/Petraeus1.pdf (as of September 12, 2006).

Pew Global Attitudes Project, *The Great Divide: How Westerners and Muslims View Each Other*, June 22, 2006. Online at http://pewglobal.org/reports/display.php?ReportID=253 (as of August 2, 2006).

Program of Instruction for Counterinsurgency Operations, Ft. Bragg, N.C.: United States Special Warfare School, 1962.

Ronfeldt, David, "Al Qaeda and Its Affiliates: A Global Tribe Waging Segmental Warfare?" *First Monday*, Vol. 10, No. 3, March 2005. Online at http://firstmonday.org/issues/issue10_3/ronfeldt/index.html (as of March 29, 2006).

Roy, Olivier, *Globalized Islam: The Search for a New Ummah*, New York: Columbia University Press, 2006.

Rumsfeld, Donald H., "Statement of Secretary of Defense Donald H. Rumsfeld, FY 2007 Posture Statement Before the House Armed Services Committee," Washington, D.C.: U.S. House of Representatives, February 8, 2006. Online at http://www.house.gov/hasc/2-8-06RumsfeldTestimony.pdf (as of September 25, 2006).

Rutz, Paul X., "Giambastiani: Conventional Trident Missiles Will Aid Terror War," *American Forces Information Service*, June 8, 2006. Online at http://www.defenselink.mil/news/Jun2006/20060608_5366.html (as of June 16, 2006).

Scheuer, Michael, *Imperial Hubris: Why the West is Losing the War on Terror*, Dulles, Va.: Brassey's, Inc., 2004.

Shadid, Anthony, "Smoke of Iraq War 'Drifting Over to Lebanon,'" *Washington Post*, June 12, 2006 p. A1.

Shea, Nina, "This Is a Saudi Textbook (After the Intolerance Was Removed)," *Washington Post*, May 21, 2006), p. B1.

Sorenson, John L., and David K. Pack, *Applied Analysis of Unconventional Warfare*, China Lake, Calif.: U.S. Naval Ordnance Test Station, April 1964.

U.S. Department of Defense, *Quadrennial Defense Review 2006*, Washington, D.C.: U.S. Government Printing Office, February 6, 2006.

Whitlock, Craig, "Architect of New War on the West," *Washington Post*, May 23, 2006, p. A1.

Windrem, Robert, "The Frightening Evolution of al-Qaida," *MSNBC.com*, June 25, 2005. Online at http://www.msnbc.msn.com/id/8307333/ (as of June 9, 2006).

Wright, Lawrence, "The Master Plan," *New Yorker*, September 11, 2006, p. 56. Online at http://www.newyorker.com/fact/content/articles/060911fa_fact3 (as of September 25, 2006).

Zogby International, *American Muslim Poll 2004: Muslims In The American Public Square: Shifting Political Winds and Fallout from 9/11, Afghanistan, and Iraq*, October 2004. Online at http://www.projectmaps.com/AMP2004report.pdf (as of August 2, 2006).